An Analysis of

Saba Mahmood's

Politics of Piety:
The Islamic Revival and
the Feminist Subject

Jessica Johnson
with
Ian S. Fairweather

Published by Macat International Ltd
24:13 Coda Centre, 189 Munster Road, London SW6 6AW.

Distributed exclusively by Routledge
2 Park Square, Milton Park, Abingdon, Oxon OX14 4RN
711 Third Avenue, New York, NY 10017, USA

Routledge is an imprint of the Taylor & Francis Group, an informa business

www.macat.com
info@macat.com

Cataloguing in Publication Data
A catalogue record for this book is available from the British Library.
Library of Congress Cataloguing-in-Publication Data is available upon request.
Cover illustration: Etienne Gilfillan

ISBN 978-1-912302-11-6 (hardback)
ISBN 978-1-912128-54-9 (paperback)
ISBN 978-1-912128-36-5 (e-book)

Notice
The information in this book is designed to orientate readers of the work under analysis,
to elucidate and contextualise its key ideas and themes, and to aid in the development
of critical thinking skills. It is not meant to be used, nor should it be used, as a
substitute for original thinking or in place of original writing or research. References and
notes are provided for informational purposes and their presence does not constitute
endorsement of the information or opinions therein. This book is presented solely for
educational purposes. It is sold on the understanding that the publisher is not engaged
to provide any scholarly advice. The publisher has made every effort to ensure that
this book is accurate and up-to-date, but makes no warranties or representations with
regard to the completeness or reliability of the information it contains. The information
and the opinions provided herein are not guaranteed or warranted to produce particular
results and may not be suitable for students of every ability. The publisher shall not be
liable for any loss, damage or disruption arising from any errors or omissions, or from
the use of this book, including, but not limited to, special, incidental, consequential or
other damages caused, or alleged to have been caused, directly or indirectly, by the
information contained within.

CONTENTS

THE MACAT LIBRARY

The Macat Library is a series of unique academic explorations of seminal works in the humanities and social sciences – books and papers that have had a significant and widely recognised impact on their disciplines. It has been created to serve as much more than just a summary of what lies between the covers of a great book. It illuminates and explores the influences on, ideas of, and impact of that book. Our goal is to offer a learning resource that encourages critical thinking and fosters a better, deeper understanding of important ideas.

Each publication is divided into three Sections: Influences, Ideas, and Impact. Each Section has four Modules. These explore every important facet of the work, and the responses to it.

This Section-Module structure makes a Macat Library book easy to use, but it has another important feature. Because each Macat book is written to the same format, it is possible (and encouraged!) to cross-reference multiple Macat books along the same lines of inquiry or research. This allows the reader to open up interesting interdisciplinary pathways.

To further aid your reading, lists of glossary terms and people mentioned are included at the end of this book (these are indicated by an asterisk [*] throughout) – as well as a list of works cited.

Macat has worked with the University of Cambridge to identify the elements of critical thinking and understand the ways in which six different skills combine to enable effective thinking.
Three allow us to fully understand a problem; three more give us the tools to solve it. Together, these six skills make up the **PACIER** model of critical thinking. They are:

ANALYSIS – understanding how an argument is built
EVALUATION – exploring the strengths and weaknesses of an argument
INTERPRETATION – understanding issues of meaning

CREATIVE THINKING – coming up with new ideas and fresh connections
PROBLEM-SOLVING – producing strong solutions
REASONING – creating strong arguments

To find out more, visit **WWW.MACAT.COM.**

CRITICAL THINKING AND *THE POLITICS OF PIETY*

Primary critical thinking skill: EVALUATION
Secondary critical thinking skill: INTERPRETATION

Saba Mahmood's 2005 *Politics of Piety* is an excellent example of evaluation in action.

Mahmood's book is a study of women's participation in the Islamic revival across the Middle East. Mahmood – a feminist social anthropologist with left-wing, secular political values – wanted to understand why women should become such active participants in a movement that seemingly promoted their subjugation. As Mahmood observed, women's active participation in the conservative Islamic revival presented (and presents) a difficult question for Western feminists: how to balance cultural sensitivity and promotion of religious freedom and pluralism with the feminist project of women's liberation? Mahmood's response was to conduct a detailed evaluation of the arguments made by both sides, examining, in particular, the reasoning of female Muslims themselves. In a key moment of evaluation, Mahmood suggests that Western feminist notions of agency are inadequate to arguments about female Muslim piety. Where Western feminists often restrict definitions of women's agency to acts that undermine the normal, male-dominated order of things, Mahmood suggests, instead, that agency can encompass female acts that uphold apparently patriarchal values.

Ultimately the Western feminist framework is, in her evaluation, inadequate and insufficient for discussing women's groups in the Islamic revival.

ABOUT THE AUTHOR OF THE ORIGINAL WORK

Saba Mahmood was born in Pakistan in 1962. As a young woman, she became interested in the relationship between Islam and politics and saw herself as a left-wing feminist, opposing the Islamification of the country imposed by the military dictator, Zia-ul-Haq. Mahmood moved to the United States in the 1980s and practiced architecture before turning first to political studies and finally to anthropology. She is now associate professor of sociocultural anthropology at University of California, Berkeley, and specializes in the anthropology of gender, religion, ethics, and the Middle East.

ABOUT THE AUTHOR OF THE ANALYSIS

Dr Jessica Johnson holds a PhD in social anthropology from the University of Cambridge and is currently a lecturer at the Department of African Studies and Anthropology at the University of Birmingham. Her research focuses on Southern Africa, in particular the anthropology of gender and law in Malawi.

Dr Ian Fairweather is lecturer in social anthropology at the University of Manchester. His research focuses on religious behavior and on the ways in which contemporary postcolonial identity strategies are articulated performatively.

ABOUT MACAT

GREAT WORKS FOR CRITICAL THINKING

Macat is focused on making the ideas of the world's great thinkers accessible and comprehensible to everybody, everywhere, in ways that promote the development of enhanced critical thinking skills.

It works with leading academics from the world's top universities to produce new analyses that focus on the ideas and the impact of the most influential works ever written across a wide variety of academic disciplines. Each of the works that sit at the heart of its growing library is an enduring example of great thinking. But by setting them in context – and looking at the influences that shaped their authors, as well as the responses they provoked – Macat encourages readers to look at these classics and game-changers with fresh eyes. Readers learn to think, engage and challenge their ideas, rather than simply accepting them.

'Macat offers an amazing first-of-its-kind tool for interdisciplinary learning and research. Its focus on works that transformed their disciplines and its rigorous approach, drawing on the world's leading experts and educational institutions, opens up a world-class education to anyone.'

Andreas Schleicher,
Director for Education and Skills, Organisation for Economic
Co-operation and Development

'Macat is taking on some of the major challenges in university education ... They have drawn together a strong team of active academics who are producing teaching materials that are novel in the breadth of their approach.'

Prof Lord Broers,
former Vice-Chancellor of the University of Cambridge

'The Macat vision is exceptionally exciting. It focuses upon new modes of learning which analyse and explain seminal texts which have profoundly influenced world thinking and so social and economic development. It promotes the kind of critical thinking which is essential for any society and economy. This is the learning of the future.'

Rt Hon Charles Clarke, former UK Secretary of State for Education

'The Macat analyses provide immediate access to the critical conversation surrounding the books that have shaped their respective discipline, which will make them an invaluable resource to all of those, students and teachers, working in the field.'

Professor William Tronzo, University of California at San Diego

WAYS IN TO THE TEXT

KEY POINTS

- Born in 1962, Saba Mahmood is a Pakistani cultural anthropologist* (someone who studies human cultures and societies). She now works in the US.

- *Politics of Piety* (2005) argues that not all women aspire to the feminist* goals of freedom and equality, and this is particularly true of those who are part of religious movements that encourage submission to male authority.

- *Politics of Piety* stands out because it describes the experiences of women in the Islamic piety movement* in Cairo from their own point of view rather than from that of a liberal outsider.

Who Is Saba Mahmood?

Saba Mahmood, the author of *Politics of Piety* (2005), is associate professor of cultural anthropology* at the University of California, Berkeley, in the United States. Born in 1962, she grew up in Pakistan, then a young and developing Muslim nation. She became interested in the relationship between Islam and politics in the postcolonial* world (that is, in nations dealing with the legacies of foreign colonialism); as a feminist intellectual—engaged with the political and cultural currents surrounding the movement for equality between men and women—she took an interest in progressive left-wing politics and opposed the introduction of laws that discriminated against women in the name of Islam.

At the time, traditionalist Islamic movements were becoming the voices of political dissent in many Muslim countries. The military dictator Zia-ul-Haq* in Pakistan, in power from 1977 to 1988, and the leaders of the successful Iranian Revolution of 1978–79* both introduced a policy of "Islamizing" their countries, so that their institutions and society reflected religious law and thought. The increasingly powerful oil-rich nations—such as Saudi Arabia, Kuwait, and the United Arab Emirates—opposed left-wing policies. Many feminists and liberals* thought that these factors, together with a lack of education, were the reasons behind the rise of Islamism.*

Mahmood, however, was not satisfied by these explanations.

On moving to the United States, she practiced architecture before becoming involved in protest against US foreign policy, particularly when the First Gulf War* began in 1990 following the US-led military response to the invasion of Kuwait by its neighbor, Iraq. She began to ask questions about the changing political and social landscape of the Muslim world and, as a first step, enrolled on a political science graduate program. However, when this failed to help her explore the question of cultural difference, she changed to anthropology.

Politics of Piety is based on Mahmood's doctoral work, completed at Stanford University and including long-term fieldwork between 1995 and 1997. Rather than return to Pakistan she did this fieldwork in Egypt to allow her some critical distance from her subjects. *Politics of Piety,* and the questions it raises about the relationship between religion, politics, and freedom, has been important to Mahmood's early career and the book established her as a major force in the anthropology of gender, religion, ethics, and the Middle East.

What Does *Politics of Piety* Say?

Politics of Piety is an original study of a particular Muslim women's movement in Cairo, the capital of Egypt, forming part of the wider Islamic revival.* The book has been influential—bringing the relationship between religion, morality, and ethical behavior to the forefront of the study of Islamic societies. It has made an important contribution to gender studies* and feminist theory.

Politics of Piety was first published in 2005 in the United States. After the terror attacks of September 11, 2001,* in which Islamic terrorists flew jet aircraft into the twin towers of the World Trade Center in New York, a climate of fear had emerged around Islam. Military interventions by the US and its allies took place in Muslim countries under the title of "the War on Terror"* and wider discussions took place in the West about various aspects of Islam, including the seemingly subordinate position it gives to women. Since then, there have been many political uprisings in the Muslim world; these have made the book even more relevant. Readers are likely to bring new and different questions to the book on account of these events.

The book was reissued in paperback in 2012, with a new preface about recent political developments in Egypt, having earlier been translated into French in 2009—at a time when the veiling of Muslim women had become a matter of considerable public interest. The French government had passed a law in 2004 banning the veil in schools; the media presented the veil as an infringement of women's rights, while the Muslim community saw the ban as preventing them from practicing their religion.

The core question in *Politics of Piety* is: why do women participate in a religious movement that encourages them to submit to male authority? In the eyes of the West, Muslim women appear to be contributing to their own powerlessness. Mahmood does not believe they accept this role simply because they are products of a male-dominated culture, however. She examines female Muslim practices that may look to the Western eye like passivity and docility, such as wearing the veil or casting down one's eyes when addressing a man.

Her conclusion is that women act in this way not because Muslim men demand it, but because they want to embody such Islamic attitudes as "modesty"—this behavior makes them virtuous Muslims in their own right.

If women's involvement in the Islamic revival has been much less extensively studied than that of men, this is partly because the West sees this as a movement that is ultimately detrimental to women, opposing the increasing influence of feminist thought. Mahmood challenges her readers to reconsider this viewpoint, particularly ideas about gender equality and individual freedom and whether they can be applied everywhere. She explores these ideas in her descriptions of women who come together to teach and study Islamic scripture, social practices, and forms of personal conduct.

Why Does *Politics of Piety* Matter?

Politics of Piety is not about the oppression or submission of Muslim women. Mahmood focuses instead on how practices like veiling or weeping during ritual prayers are a way for women to achieve an ideal of Muslim virtue. Mahmood does not try to produce an alternative universal theory of women's agency*—their ability to act independently in the world. In fact, *Politics of Piety* argues against universal theorizing and Mahmood questions the relevance to the women she studies of Western feminism, with its goals of universal freedom and equality. She also refuses to assess these women according to feminist principles or liberal expectations that they do not share.

Mahmood's work is an important example of a contemporary approach to anthropology and her long-term fieldwork in a local setting has given her sensitivity to local aspirations. Nowadays, most anthropologists are increasingly wary of generalizing: they avoid applying ideas derived from one setting uncritically to other parts of the world. This is a crucial point for the reader of contemporary anthropology.

Since *Politics of Piety* was first published, there have been several plitical uprisings in Egypt, the wider Arab Spring* and more recently the rise of the militant organization ISIL* ("The Islamic State of Iraq and the Levant") and the departure of certain young Western Muslims who want to join them fighting for territory in Iraq and Syria and elsewhere. All of this has contributed to the increased interest in the political movement known as Islamism, which is founded on the principle, roughly, that Islam is the best model for government. This is a theme central to Mahmood's text. Images of veiled Muslim women in the media generate a negative response—one of many negative influences on public opinion in the US and other Western nations.

The importance of Mahmood's discussion of Islamic practices reaches beyond anthropology and gender studies. As Western feminist arguments increasingly contribute to Western political attitudes about Islamic societies, there is a need for more sensitive assessments of the lives of Muslim women. *Politics of Piety* makes an important contribution to this. It broadens our understanding of the Islamic faith, which—in turn—helps to combat what Mahmood regards as the ill-informed and irrational views about Muslims that have bolstered support for military interventions in recent years.

SECTION 1
INFLUENCES

MODULE 1
THE AUTHOR AND THE HISTORICAL CONTEXT

KEY POINTS

- *Politics of Piety* remains relevant given the continuing tensions between Islamic and Western societies and the potential for misunderstanding and misrepresentation.
- Mahmood's work was shaped by her experience as a feminist* scholar in Muslim Pakistan and her subsequent long-term fieldwork in Egypt.
- She was profoundly affected by the events of September 11, 2001,* the subsequent climate of fear, and the continued distrust of Muslims.

Why Read this Text?

Saba Mahmood's 2005 book *Politics of Piety: The Islamic Revival and the Feminist Subject* challenges the view, commonly held in the West, that women in Muslim societies are passive victims of a patriarchal* culture (that is, that they are subject to life in a culture defined by a system of male dominance). The book has been influential within the discipline of social and cultural anthropology* and beyond, winning the 2005 Victoria Shuck Award of the American Political Science Association, and achieving an Honorable Mention as part of the 2005 Albert Hourani Book Award of the Middle East Studies Association.

In *Politics of Piety,* Mahmood gives a nuanced and sensitive account of women within an Islamic piety movement* in Cairo (a society of women who meet to study scripture and social practices considered essential to the achievement of virtuousness). Her key interests in gender, Islam, and ethics have all attracted a considerable amount of

> **❝** I have come to believe that a certain amount of self-scrutiny and skepticism is essential regarding the certainty of my own political commitments, when trying to understand the lives of others who do not necessarily share these commitments. **❞**
>
> Saba Mahmood, *Politics of Piety: The Islamic Revival and the Feminist Subject*

attention among anthropologists in recent years. In particular, she has made an important anthropological point by questioning Western scholars who examine gender issues in Islam with a traditional Western liberal* feminist agenda.

After the attacks on the World Trade Centre in 2001 by Al Qaeda* came the declared war on the politically radicalized Muslim terror groups often referred to as "Islamist";* Islam was presented in the Western media as being opposed to Western ideas of freedom. Images of veiled Muslim women became symbolic of this lack of freedom, an illustration of their supposed oppression. There was a widespread assumption that Muslim women would not choose to wear the veil and secular* feminist values became central to this discussion. This made Mahmood's challenge to political feminist thinking particularly timely.[1] *The Politics of Piety* confronts previously accepted views on Islamist movements and our understanding of the relationship between ethics and politics.

Author's Life

Saba Mahmood grew up in Pakistan, where she was involved in progressive left-wing politics. She was committed to critical Marxism* (the thought and social analysis of the German economist and political theorist Karl Marx)* and feminism and took a stand against the introduction of laws that discriminated against women in the name of

Islam.[2] She moved to the US in the 1980s and practiced architecture for four years while becoming involved in activism against US foreign policy. With her increasing interest in politics, she enrolled initially in a political science graduate program, but found it did not answer the kinds of questions that interested her and so turned to anthropology.

Mahmood's doctoral work, on which *Politics of Piety* is based, was completed at Stanford University. She is currently associate professor of sociocultural anthropology at University of California, Berkeley. Her background and experience in Pakistan profoundly shaped her interest in Islamic politics. She began to investigate the role of Islamic movements as the principal political opposition in a number of Muslim countries and how their rise challenged ideals of secular nationalism.*

In her preface to *Politics of Piety*, Mahmood explains that she chose to work in Egypt and not her native Pakistan to give herself the political and intellectual distance she needed.[3] Mahmood's starting point was her faith in secular liberal feminism, its goals of female equality and freedom, and the idea that they applied to all women. But this belief was shaken by her experiences during fieldwork in Egypt. As she came to understand how the women she studied conducted their lives and performed their faith, she began to question the mainstream feminist viewpoint about women's resistance to patriarchal society.

Author's Background

While Mahmood began working as a secular liberal feminist scholar, she became increasingly dissatisfied with the explanations given by this school of thought about the return to Islamic doctrines and traditional social norms in many Muslim countries. This viewpoint tended to attribute such developments to a lack of education, or resentment about the involvement of the US in the Middle East. However, Mahmood thought these explanations failed to take account of the variety of Islamic revival* movements and their appeal to the educated middle classes.[4]

It is significant that the text was written after the Al Qaeda* attacks on New York and Washington, DC. Mahmood believed the attacks resulted in a climate of fear and anti-Islamic sentiment and a mainstream view of Islam and its adherents as dangerously irrational.[5] The subsequent military campaign by the United States and its allies in the "War on Terror"* accelerated her efforts to explain the relationship between Islam and politics and fueled her desire to give a deeper understanding of the Islamic faith.

The text was reissued in paperback in 2012 when Egypt was undergoing momentous political change following the wave of demonstrations and protests known as the Arab Spring* that began in Tunisia in 2010 and spread throughout the Arab world, leading to the overthrow of the Egyptian president Hosni Mubarak.* More than four years on, upheaval continues in Egypt, with Islamist movements taking center stage and making Mahmood's study of the relationship between Islam and politics all the more relevant.

NOTES

1   Sindre Bangstad, "Saba Mahmood and Anthropological Feminism After Virtue *Theory," in Culture & Society* vol. 28, no. 3 (2011): 29.

2   Saba Mahmood, *Politics of Piety: The Islamic Revival and the Feminist Subject* (Princeton University Press, 2005), ix.

3   Mahmood, *Politics of Piety*, xxiv.

4   Mahmood, *Politics of Piety*, x.

5   Mahmood, *Politics of Piety*, 1.

MODULE 2
ACADEMIC CONTEXT

KEY POINTS

- Anthropology questions assumptions that are taken for granted within one culture by examining them from the point of view of another culture.

- Anthropologists have more in common with the views of other philosophers, such as the ancient Greek philosopher Aristotle,* the French thinker and social theorist Michel Foucault,* and the Canadian philosopher Charles Taylor* who believe the actions of individuals must be influenced by the culture in which they live. Mahmood uses these philosophical approaches to agency* (our capacity to act) to develop her critique of secular liberal feminism.*

- *Politics of Piety* questions assumptions about the passivity of Muslim women. The work is influenced by approaches used in anthropology and analyses of society that challenge the assumptions of Western liberal thought.

The Work In Its Context

Saba Mahmood's *Politics of Piety* is a work of anthropology—a discipline in which researchers investigate assumptions otherwise taken for granted by adopting the perspective of another culture. This cross-cultural approach remains at the heart of the discipline;[1] accordingly, anthropologists interested in religion ask questions about the relationship between religion and other aspects of society, such as politics, across cultures, while feminist anthropologists focus on how cultural ideas about gender* shape both the behavior of the people they study and the way in which we understand it.

Anthropology avoids generalizations about "Islam" or "women,"

> ❝ Foucault's conception of positive ethics is Aristotelian in that it conceives of ethics not as an Idea, or as a set of regulatory norms, but as a set of practical activities that are germane to a certain way of life. Ethics in this conception is embedded in a set of specific practices (what Aristotle called 'practices of virtue'). ❞
>
> Saba Mahmood, *Politics of Piety: The Islamic Revival and the Feminist Subject*

for example, and concentrates instead on the details of particular local practices. This is the tradition in which Mahmood works, deliberately leaving open the possibility that both her own and her readers' perspectives "might also be unmade in the process of engaging another's worldview, that we might come to learn things that we did not already know before we undertook the engagement."[2]

A key concern for anthropologists is: how much do individuals act according to their own desires or are their thoughts and actions constrained by their culture? That is, are individuals really free agents? The term agency* is used in anthropology and other social sciences to mean the ability of a person (sometimes referred to as an "agent") to act without constraint in the world.

Overview of the Field

The study of agency in anthropology originates in a philosophical approach to ethics attributed to the ancient Greek philosopher Aristotle. For Aristotle, to live a "good" ethical life required particular habits or "virtues" that could only be acquired by following certain outward practices and ways of behaving. Culture, though, can influence how we behave in society, and so affect the type of ethical agent an individual can be.

The French philosopher Michel Foucault*[3] is also of interest to anthropologists who study the ideas of Aristotle, as he similarly prioritized practice. He saw ethics not simply as rules that regulate behavior, but as complex practical activities including bodily techniques—casting down the eyes when addressing men, for example, to express modesty—that define particular ways of life. Living with these practices results in highly specific moral attitudes and behaviors[4] and Mahmood's argument is that they not only express an individual's modesty but actually *form* that modesty, too.

Simply put, acting ethically makes you ethical.

The Canadian philosopher Charles Taylor* is another key figure at the meeting point of anthropology and ethics. Taylor is known for questioning liberal notions of the self[5] that assume the idea that the self is independent from the body and existed prior to any social experience. As a communitarian,* however, and so someone who puts great weight on the individual's connection with the community, Taylor seeks to focus on the social institutions and contexts in which lives are lived and have meaning. It is this emphasis on the social context of action that is so in tune with the viewpoint of anthropology.

Academic Influences

Two influential works reveal the importance of agency in feminist anthropology. The first is the Canadian anthropologist Janice Boddy's* book *Wombs and Alien Spirits: Women, Men and the Zar Cult in Northern Sudan*,[6] which describes a women's healing cult in an Arabic-speaking region of northern Sudan that Boddy sees as a form of resistance to male authority.

The second is the anthropologist Lila Abu-Lughod* of Colombia University's study *Veiled Sentiments: Honor and Poetry in a Bedouin Society*,[7] an account of how women's poetry in a Bedouin tribe constitutes a socially acceptable vehicle for their protest against male domination.

Boddy and Abu-Lughod's work challenged the usual portrayal of

Arab and Muslim women as passive and submissive. They analyzed the way the women expressed resistance to the strict rules that regulated their lives so that the women's own voices could be heard. These authors share an interpretation of agency as referring to "political and moral autonomy"[8]—that within the law, individuals can act according to their own free will.

Essentially, we are "free agents." While this view represents an advance over earlier approaches, this concept of agency is mostly concerned with power and resistance.

In *Politics of Piety: The Islamic Revival and the Feminist Subject,* Saba Mahmood extends the theoretical work of Foucault and Taylor beyond their original settings and arguments. Her work belongs within a body of work challenging the assumptions of liberalism,* an emerging field of anthropology considered to be at the cutting edge of theoretical trends in the study of gender, citizenship, and embodiment*—or experiencing your self through the body and not just the mind.

Mahmood also participated (with others such as the anthropologist Elizabeth Povinelli)[9] in the Late Liberalism Project,* a forum for discussion that focused on confrontations and conflicts between liberal ideas and indigenous people, sexual or religious minorities or, in Mahmood's case, Muslim women. These points of conflict allow anthropologists to see liberalism from beyond its own terms of reference.

NOTES

1   George Marcus and Michael Fischer, eds., *Anthropology as Cultural Critique: An Experimental Moment in the Human Sciences* (Chicago: University of Chicago Press, 1986), 20.

2   Saba Mahmood, *Politics of Piety: The Islamic Revival and the Feminist Subject* (Princeton: Princeton University Press, 2005), 36–37.

3   See especially Michel Foucault, *The History of Sexuality, Vol. 2: The Use of Pleasure*, trans. R. Hurley (London: Penguin Books, 1985).

4   Mahmood, *Politics of Piety*, 28.

5   See especially Charles Taylor, "Atomism," in *Philosophy and the Human Sciences: Philosophical Papers 2* (Cambridge: Cambridge University Press, 1985), 187–210; and "What's Wrong with Negative Liberty?" in *Philosophy and the Human Sciences*, 211–29.

6   Janice Boddy, *Wombs and Alien Spirits: Women, Men, and the Zar Cult in Northern Sudan* (Madison: University of Wisconsin Press, 1989).

7   Lila Abu-Lughod, *Veiled Sentiments: Honor and Poetry in a Bedouin Society* (Berkeley: University of California Press, 1986).

8   Mahmood, *Politics of Piety*, 7.

9   Elizabeth A. Povinelli, *Economies of Abandonment: Social Belonging and Endurance in Late Liberalism* (Durham, NC: Duke University Press, 2011).

MODULE 3
THE PROBLEM

KEY POINTS

- Feminist* scholars wanted to understand the nature of women's agency*—their ability to act independently—when women's actions appeared to support their own subordination.

- They challenged the view that Muslim women were passive victims of male domination and their behavior was the result of socialization.

- Mahmood rejected the idea that women's agency can only be seen in resistance to patriarchal norms* such as wearing the veil, being modest, and obeying men.

Core Question

Saba Mahmood's *Politics of Piety: The Islamic Revival and the Feminist Subject* was an important part of the debate about how to understand female agency in Muslim contexts. She was writing at a time when images of veiled Muslim women were widespread in the Western media and often interpreted as evidence of the women's passivity and subordination.

This view supported the influential "clash of civilizations" theory in international relations associated with the conservative political theorist Samuel Huntingdon.* Huntingdon saw Islam and "the West" as fundamentally different "civilizations" locked in a deadly power struggle.[1] Highlighting the subordination of Muslim women gave support to interventions that, in the long run, it was hoped, would bring about the spread of democracy and promote the rights of the individual in line with the liberal* model.

> **"** What may appear to be a case of deplorable passivity and docility from a progressivist point of view, may actually be a form of agency ... In this sense, agential capacity is entailed not only in those acts that resist norms but also in the multiple ways in which one *inhabits* norms. **"**
>
> Saba Mahmood, *Politics of Piety: The Islamic Revival and the Feminist Subject*

For feminist scholars, working with the social and cultural perspectives associated with the wider movement towards equality between the sexes, the important questions concerned how women came to actively contribute to their own subordination. Western secular liberal feminists* understand religion as a matter of individual choice. They see freedom as the right to fulfill one's hopes and desires. So they have difficulty coming to terms with an Islamic culture that puts a high value on submission to God's will.

They tend to understand Muslim women's compliance with the so-called "feminine virtues" of shyness, modesty, and humility, as an acceptance of patriarchal norms due to socialization.[2] That is to say, if women believe that they should behave in ways that are not in their interest (such as veiling or casting down their eyes when addressing men), they do so only because they are the products of a male-dominated culture that has taught them to believe this.

From the 1970s, however, some scholars sought to "restore" women's voices and turned their attention to how women resist or subvert patriarchal norms in line with their "own interests and agendas."[3] This idea of women's "own interests and agendas" became a new focus for study.

The Participants

The debate about agency has been dominated by two philosophical approaches to ethics. The first, known as virtue ethics,* can be traced back to the Greek philosopher Aristotle,* who insisted that ethics ought to be approached through human comportment (conduct) and bodily practice. The second is deontological ethics,* associated with the German philosopher Immanuel Kant*—an approach that emphasizes the role of reason.

Kant's theory was that the individual has a duty to know right from wrong and to choose the right way by his or her own free will, a view that has been fundamental to the development of liberal thought. Kant held that ethics was a matter of reason and not connected to a social context. He argued that an action could only be ethical if it was a product of reason: that is, one must choose to act ethically in spite of one's inclinations, habits, and disposition.[4]

An act can be ethical, according to Kant, only if it is a conscious decision and not if it is performed unconsciously or out of habit.

Kant's impact upon European thought has been significant and the notion of the ethical subject*—someone who acts according to his or her free will—is at the heart of liberal understandings of the self. By emphasizing the will, the responsibility for ethical agency lies with the individual rather than his or her culture.

The French social theorist Michel Foucault,* though, subsequently revived interest in Aristotle's virtue ethics by bringing into view "the careful scrutiny one applies to one's daily actions in order to shape oneself to live in accordance with a particular model of behavior."[5] For Foucault, ethics are not just rules but practical activities that define a moral way of life—what Aristotle called "practices of virtue."

The Contemporary Debate

Mahmood acknowledges the influence of the feminist scholar Judith Butler,* who was one of her mentors. Butler encouraged Mahmood to engage with feminist theory and consider the relationship between feminist scholarship and politics.

Her book *Gender Trouble: Feminism and the Subversion of Identity*[6] gives an insight into Mahmood's argument in the *Politics of Piety.* Butler applied Foucault's argument to the idea of women's agency, insisting that the ability of women to act must be understood in relation to the patriarchal norms that determine their everyday ethical practices and mold them as ethical subjects ("patriarchal norms" referring to the behavior considered appropriate in a culture defined by male power).

This argument was developed further by the anthropologist Lila Abu-Lughod,* who argued that women find ways to subvert the meanings of cultural and religious practices to resist the dominant male order and assert their own "agency."[7] Mahmood goes further than these authors, however, by arguing that the traditional view that relates agency to resistance does not work in the context of an Islamic piety movement.*

Another of Mahmood's mentors is the anthropologist Talal Asad,* who has written extensively on postcolonialism (the various legacies of colonialism, in thought, culture, and politics), Islam, and Christianity.[8] Asad's essay "The Idea of an Anthropology of Islam"[9] challenged Mahmood to ask questions about Islam and religion in general. Indeed, Mahmood's approach to the study of Islam is often said to bear the imprint of Asad's scholarship, not least the importance he attached to understanding the contexts of Islamic knowledge founded upon the Koran* (the text central to the Islamic religion) and the Hadith* (a body of writings reporting the Prophet Muhammad's statements).

NOTES

1   Samuel Huntington, *The Clash of Civilizations and the Remaking of World Order* (London: Simon and Schuster, 2002), 238.

2   Saba Mahmood, *Politics of Piety: The Islamic Revival and the Feminist Subject* (Princeton: Princeton University Press, 2005), 6.

3   Mahmood, *Politics of Piety*, 6.

4   Immanuel Kant, "The Metaphysics of Morals," *in Practical Philosophy: The Cambridge Edition of the Works of Immanuel Kant*, trans. and ed. Mary J. Gregor (Cambridge: Cambridge University Press, 1996), 67–68.

5   Mahmood, *Politics of Piety*, 187.

6   Judith Butler, *Gender Trouble: Feminism and the Subversion of Identity* (London: Routledge, 1989).

7   Lila Abu-Lughod, *Veiled Sentiments: Honor and Poetry in a Bedouin Society* (Berkeley: University of California Press, 1986).

8   See especially Talal Asad, *Genealogies of Religion: Discipline and Reasons of Power in Christianity and Islam* (Baltimore: Johns Hopkins University Press, 1993) and *Formations of the Secular: Christianity, Islam, Modernity* (Stanford: Stanford University Press, 2003).

9   Talal Asad, *The Idea of an Anthropology of Islam*, Occasional Papers Series (Washington, DC: Center for Contemporary Arab Studies, Georgetown University, 1986).

THE AUTHOR'S CONTRIBUTION

KEY POINTS

- When women support religious principles that contribute to their own subordination, Mahmood believed their agency* (independent action) could be seen in the ways they find to make cultural norms their own.

- This view challenged the notion that Western ideas about female equality and freedom could be applied to all women and highlighted the problems that occur when they are imposed on other cultures.

- Mahmood's point of view developed the earlier work of feminist scholars and anthropologists such as Judith Butler* and Lila Abu-Lughod.*

Author's Aims

In *Politics of Piety: The Islamic Revival and the Feminist Subject,* Saba Mahmood's response to the debate about agency among feminists* and anthropologists was to move it on. Her aim was to get away from glorifying particular instances of female "resistance" against male-dominated cultures; instead, she wanted to understand why women would willingly take part in a movement that encourages them to submit to male authority.

Her research centered on the Islamic piety movement* (societies made up of women from a broad range of socioeconomic backgrounds who met regularly in mosques across the city of Cairo to study Islamic scripture and learn the social practices and forms of behavior they considered essential to the development of the ideal virtuous self*—in this case, the good Muslim woman). The women at the heart of Mahmood's study supported religious principles that included female

> 66 Does a commitment to the idea of equality in our own lives endow us with the capacity to know that this ideal captures what is or should be fulfilling for everyone else? If it does not, as is surely the case, then I think we need to rethink, with far more humility than we are accustomed to, what feminist politics really means. 99
>
> Saba Mahmood, *Politics of Piety: The Islamic Revival and the Feminist Subject*

subordination, which posed a dilemma for feminist analysis; but despite the constraints the women faced, Mahmood maintains that their lives and choices "must be explored on their own terms if one is to understand the structuring conditions of this form of ethical life and the forms of agency they entail."[1]

Mahmood's innovation was to make her readers reconsider what such key concepts as autonomy* (our ability to act independently), freedom, and ethics actually mean, and she questioned the usual interpretations of movements whose foundations lay outside the liberal* West. Her alternative understanding of agency argues that in the case of the women she studied, agency can be seen in how they uphold such forms of behavior as modesty and shyness that she calls "norms."*

Approach

Mahmood's originality in *Politics of Piety* lies in the way she draws insights from a diverse range of scholarly inquiry. She takes anthropology's traditional stance of humility about other people's cultures, but she extends this to feminist politics. Her ethnographic* account (that is, the written record of her research) of an urban women's piety movement reveals the movement's historical significance. This was the first time that women had come together in public meetings on such a scale to teach one another Islamic scripture in mosques, "thereby altering the historically male-centered character of mosques as well as Islamic pedagogy"[2] (that is, methods of teaching). The women studied Islamic texts and taught each other, focusing on social practices and forms of bodily comportment, such as wearing the veil and modest demeanor.[3] They debated how to incorporate ideals about women's modesty, including wearing the veil, into their everyday modern situations.

Mahmood's approach to the women of the piety movement was, in the best spirit of ethnography, to remain open. She worked on the basis that her own ideas about gender and politics might be informed and changed by her fieldwork.[4] This turned out to be the case. She ultimately challenges the idea that the liberal view on female equality and freedom can be applied to all women and shows that such views cannot be imposed on other cultures.

Contribution in Context

Mahmood's work takes place in a very specific context. Anthropologists and feminist scholars were becoming increasingly interested in the Greek philosopher Aristotle's* notion of virtue ethics* as developed in the work of the French social theorist Michel Foucault* and the Canadian philosopher Charles Taylor.* In what is sometimes known as the "ethical turn"* in anthropology,[5] scholars favored virtue ethics (which focuses on bodily practices through which the ideal virtual self—the model of ethical behavior—is cultivated) rather than the German philosopher Kant's* deontological* understanding of ethics (which emphasizes the importance of the will in choosing to behave ethically).

In advocating virtue ethics Mahmood explains: "An inquiry into ethics from this perspective requires that one examine not simply the values enshrined in moral codes, but the different ways in which people live these codes—something anthropologists are uniquely situated to observe."[6] Mahmood goes on to argue that the Kantian emphasis on the will in most Western theories of ethics has led to a failure to pay attention "to the manifest form ethical practices take, and a general demotion of conduct, social demeanor, and etiquettes in our analyses of moral systems."[7]

Mahmood combines this anthropological application of virtue ethics with a feminist one drawn from the work of her mentor Judith Butler,* whose work has influenced many other feminist anthropologists including Lila Abu-Lughod.* This blending of anthropology with feminist scholarship has led to much debate on gender roles in non-Western societies and understanding women's agency across cultures. This growing field of study in the developing world has led to more cultural sensitivity; traditional Western feminism—with its struggle for equal rights and opportunities—is no longer seen as necessarily relevant to all cultures.

Mahmood's assessment of secular liberal feminist assumptions has made a significant contribution to this changing viewpoint, especially in the idea that another way of having power over your own life is to make cultural norms your own.

NOTES

1 Saba Mahmood, *Politics of Piety: The Islamic Revival and the Feminist Subject* (Princeton: Princeton University Press, 2005), 187

2 Mahmood, *Politics of Piety*, 2.

3 Mahmood, *Politics of Piety*, 2.

4 Mahmood, *Politics of Piety*, 37.

5 See Didier Fassin, "The Ethical Turn in Anthropology: Promises and Uncertainties," in *Hau: Journal of Ethnographic Theory* vol. 4, no. 1 (2014): 429–35.

6 Mahmood, *Politics of Piety*, 120.

7 Mahmood, *Politics of Piety*, 26.

SECTION 2
IDEAS

MAIN IDEAS

KEY POINTS

- The main ideas in *Politics of Piety* are freedom and agency,* ethics, gender politics, and Islamic revival.*

- The main argument is that women can have control over their own lives both in the way they live in a patriarchal* society and in how they resist its norms.*

- Mahmood uses her close analysis of a women's Islamic piety movement* in Cairo to make this argument and to give a voice to the women she studied.

Key Themes

Saba Mahmood's *Politics of Piety: The Islamic Revival and the Feminist Subject* is a book about women's involvement in the Islamic revival taking place in Egypt and across the Arab world. The Islamic revival loosely refers to the development since the 1970s of a "back to basics" form of Islam and takes different forms around the Islamic world. While these revivals are all motivated by a wish to make Muslim values central to daily life, they can range from peacefully persuading people to be more pious to, at the other extreme, Islamist* campaigns aiming to establish Islamic states under Sharia law* that resort to violence or terror.

There has been much less study of women's role in this revival than that of men, partly because its goals and ideals are thought to oppose the true interests of women. Mahmood, however, attended many meetings in several mosques of a women's piety movement during her fieldwork. As a result, she reassessed what a commitment to Islam means and examined the reasons why women would strive for a

> ❝ Among mosque participants, individual efforts toward self-realization are aimed not so much at discovering one's 'true' desires and feelings, or at establishing a personal relationship with God, but at honing one's rational and emotional capacities so as to approximate the exemplary model of the pious self. ❞
>
> Saba Mahmood, *Politics of Piety: The Islamic Revival and the Feminist Subject*

pious submission to patriarchal norms.

Her research showed women from a wide range of backgrounds and teachers with a wide range of views took part in the movement. There would often be a vigorous exchange of ideas and women who did not like the views of one teacher would move to another group they found more in line with their own thinking. One common factor was the emphasis put on outward behavior—what you do, rather than what you think—because virtue is derived from action, not thought. Wearing a veil is not just saying "I am modest," then; it actually makes you modest, which is the ultimate aim.

Mahmood's conclusion was that the women she studied did not value the idea of "freedom" in the same way as the liberal* West does, and that such women can give us new insights into ideas that we often take for granted about freedom and autonomy.[1]

One of Mahmood's key themes is the relationship between freedom and agency (the ability to act in the world) within the Islamic revival. She particularly wants her readers to reconsider some of the most widely held assumptions of secular liberal feminism* about freedom and the ability to act.

The question of agency is also central to Mahmood's next key theme, which is gender inequality. She argues that we have to reassess whether the goals that motivate Western feminism can be applied to all women. Broadly speaking, these goals are gender equality and individual women's freedom from constraints. The book challenges us to look beyond the assumptions and to consider the perspectives of women who do not share these ideals.

The third key theme of *Politics of Piety* is "ethical self-formation"— or how ethical action is connected to individual freedom and agency when developing the virtuous self.*

Exploring the Ideas

At the heart of *Politics of Piety* is women's participation in the piety movement and their active support for religious principles that sustain their own subordination. Mahmood believes this is best understood outside the tradition of feminist scholarship that regards resistance as the only form of independent action. Mahmood believes, though, that action can also be seen in the ways women uphold and perpetuate forms of behavior that she calls "norms,"* or patriarchal norms.

As an example, Mahmood discusses the Islamic virtue of female modesty. Many of the participants in the mosque movement believe that wearing the veil both expresses modesty and is a means of acquiring it. As they see it, bodily behavior (wearing the veil) does not just indicate that the woman is modest, but is essential to her becoming modest. The veiled body is the means through which modesty is both created and expressed.[2]

Mahmood's argument rejects the deontological* understanding of ethics—that it is an effort of will that makes someone virtuous—that is at the heart of secular liberal understandings of the self. According to this viewpoint, the outward aspects of behavior such as dress or bodily comportment only matter because they reveal an internal mental state.

Mahmood argues this does not allow ethical practices their true importance.[3] As she puts it, "bodily behavior does not simply stand in a relationship of meaning to self and society, but it also endows the self with certain kinds of capacities that provide the substance from which the world is acted upon."[4] Patriarchal norms are, therefore, more than a mere social imposition on the individual. They determine the everyday conduct, dress, and bodily comportment of a woman, whether she upholds or resists them, and play a vital part in her life as an ethical and political agent.

Language and Expression

Mahmood was writing primarily for an educated Western audience, not specifically for anthropologists but also for philosophers and, especially, feminist scholars. She writes on the basis that the majority of her readership will have limited firsthand experience of the Islamic revival but will be familiar with the attitudes of the period following September 11, 2001,* when fear and suspicion of Muslims, as well as disapproval of the seemingly subordinate position accorded to women within the Muslim faith, dominated Western representations of Islam.

Nevertheless, she writes in the tradition of anthropology, providing a thick description* (plentiful detail) of the texture of the lives of the women with whom she worked. She introduces individual members of the piety movement, and reveals how their solutions to the challenges of fulfilling their pious goals within their everyday realities differ and draw upon varying sources of Islamic authority.

In one example, she examines a discussion about the requirement to pray five times a day. Many of the women found this difficult to fit in around their other demands—work, children, study—and the teacher explained with reference to Islamic scripture that the more they prayed the easier they would find it to do. So, it was not just a requirement for a good Muslim. They would want to pray more—an example of right behavior leading to right attitudes.

Mahmood makes use of a number of difficult philosophical concepts in order to support her argument. The most important of these is the notion of ethical self-formation,* the process by which individuals make themselves virtuous.

The piety movement, according to Mahmood, places an extraordinary degree of emphasis on "outward markers of religiosity—ritual practices, styles of comporting oneself, dress, and so on."[5] The women regard these as necessary to become pious Muslims. They seek to model their conduct on that of the Prophet and his companions but do not see this as a constraint on their individual freedom. As Mahmood puts it "they treated socially authorized forms of performance as the potentialities—the ground if you will—through which the self is realized"[6].

This behavior and conduct can be seen as a way to develop an individual's actions, capacities, and skills for living an ethical life and these outward gestures correspond to inner states like intentions and thoughts. This is what is meant by "ethical self-formation."

NOTES

1   Saba Mahmood, *Politics of Piety: The Islamic Revival and the Feminist Subject* (Princeton University Press, 2005), 39.

2   Mahmood, *Politics of Piety*, 23.

3   Mahmood, *Politics of Piety*, 26.

4   Mahmood, *Politics of Piety*, 27.

5   Mahmood, *Politics of Piety*, 31.

6   Mahmood, *Politics of Piety*, 31.

MODULE 6
SECONDARY IDEAS

KEY POINTS

- An important secondary idea in *Politics of Piety* is that ritual is a way of developing the self as a part of everyday practice.

- This idea addresses important debates in anthropology rather than Saba Mahmood's main critique of secular liberal feminism.

- Mahmood makes an important point about ritual, redefining it as part of the process of self-development rather than a performance.

Other Ideas

An important secondary idea in Saba Mahmood's *Politics of Piety* is the relationship between religious ritual and everyday life. Anthropologists writing about ritual such as Victor Turner* and Stanley Tambiah* have made a distinction between "formal or conventional behavior, and routine, informal, or mundane activity":[1] that is, between ritual behavior and normal, daily activity.

For Tambiah, for example, ritual is a staged performance that expresses the status and interests of the participants. They are separated from their own emotions by the formulaic or stereotyped nature of the ritual itself and the public morality they must display.[2] Turner argues that the collective unconscious* is the main principle of ritual symbolism. In this, he was drawing on the psychologist Carl Jung,* who believed that the symbols used in religious rituals are powerful because we recognize them on an unconscious level even if we do not consciously know their meaning. Like Tambiah, Turner sees ritual as a

> 66 Ordinary acts 'express' attitudes and feelings directly (for example, crying denotes distress in Western society) and 'communicate' that information to interacting persons (the person crying wishes to convey to another his feeling of distress). But ritualized, conventionalized, stereotyped behavior is construed in order to express and communicate, and is publicly construed as expressing and communicating certain attitudes congenial to an ongoing institutionalized intercourse. 99
>
> Stanley Tambiah, *Culture, Thought and Social Action: An Anthropological Perspective*

performance, with the interplay of formalized and improvised elements acting as a way of rousing, channeling, and finally bringing under control powerful emotions.[3]

Mahmood encourages a rethinking of this viewpoint.[4] Defining ritual action as formal and conventional sets it apart from routine and informal activities. Mahmood argues that this does not work for the study of the piety movement* in Cairo because ritual action here *is* mundane, routine, and informal. Ritual, she argues, is one of the forums in which "the self comes to acquire and give expression to its proper form."[5]

Exploring the Ideas

Mahmood argues that the model of a "theatre in which a preformed self enacts a script of social action"[6] is not the best way to understand ritual. From this viewpoint, emotional spontaneity is controlled by the acting out of a conventional social script—and this, says Mahmood, cannot explain how women in the piety movement in Cairo approach ritual prayer. For these women, prayers are not primarily symbolic activities. She describes, for instance, how the women weep during prayer as an expression of reverence. This weeping is not provoked by personal suffering and therefore it is not a release of emotions in Victor Turner's sense, but neither is it a scripted ritual performance as Tambiah would see it. It must "issue forth out of a sense of being overwhelmed by God's greatness."[7]

The ability to cry effortlessly at the appropriate moment does not come easily, but has to be learned through the practice of ritual prayer. From this perspective, ritual does not just express inner feelings and motivations, it is a space to cultivate appropriate emotions and one of the places where the virtuous self* is formed in an intentional, conscious process.

Overlooked

Mahmood has often suggested that many of her readers overwhelmingly focus on the question of agency* and how "agents" are to be identified. In doing so, they overlook the significance of "the constructive work different conceptual understandings of a practice [veiling, for example, or relating to the Koran]* accomplish in the making of subjects and the creation of distinct social and political imaginaries."[8]

According to Tambiah, ritual performances such as praying or weeping should not be understood as a "free expression of emotions" but a disciplined practice of "right attitudes."[9] For the members of the piety movement, however, it is not enough to demonstrate the right attitude. One has to do so *spontaneously*: one's desires and emotions must conform to Islamic conventions. The women's aim was to make prescribed emotions ones that occurred naturally to them.

Rituals are a kind of discipline by which one's real feelings are brought into line with what one is supposed to feel.[10] This dissolves the distinction between stereotyped ritual behavior and spontaneous informal behavior.

Mahmood's discussion of ritual highlights the problems in anthropology's distinction between "true desires" and obligatory social acts.[11] There are implications here for liberal assumptions about politics in which conventional behavior is taken as evidence of social control and repression. Mahmood's ultimate aim was to "challenge the very assumptions on the basis of which [the members of the piety movement] are judged as passive, obsequious, and uncritical."[12]

If this aspect of Mahmood's argument has been overlooked, it is possible to speculate that this is changing. The social anthropologist Paul Anderson,* for instance, although largely supportive of Mahmood's work, criticizes how she prioritizes the way people use ritual practices as a way of working on the self. He focuses on the importance of group participation in this self-improvement work: how people encourage and admonish each other, and so on.[13]

NOTES

1   Saba Mahmood, *Politics of Piety: The Islamic Revival and the Feminist Subject* (Princeton: Princeton University Press, 2005), 127.

2   Stanley J. Tambiah, *A Performative Approach to Ritual* (London: The British Academy and Oxford University Press, 1979).

3   See especially Victor W. Turner, *The Ritual Process: Structure and Anti-Structure* (Chicago: Aldine Publishing Co., 1969).

4   Catherine Bell, *Ritual Theory, Ritual Practice* (Oxford: Oxford University Press, 1992).

5   Mahmood, *Politics of Piety*, 131.

6   Mahmood, *Politics of Piety*, 131.

7   Saba Mahmood, "Rehearsed Spontaneity and the Conventionality of Ritual: Disciplines of Salat," in *American Ethnologist* vol. 28, issue 4 (2008): 843.

8   Mahmood, *Politics of Piety*, xii.

9 Stanley Tambiah, *Culture, Thought, and Social Action: An Anthropological Perspective* (Cambridge, Mass.: Harvard University Press, 1985), 134.

10 Mahmood, "Rehearsed Spontaneity," 843.

11 Mahmood, "Rehearsed Spontaneity," 845.

12 Mahmood, *Politics of Piety*, xii.

13 Paul Anderson, "'The Piety of the Gift': Selfhood and Sociality in the Egyptian Mosque Movement," *Anthropological Theory* vol. 11, no. 1 (2011): 3–21.

MODULE 7
ACHIEVEMENT

KEY POINTS

- Mahmood's greatest achievement in *Politics of Piety* was to question the widely accepted idea that liberal feminist* goals of freedom and equality are applicable to women in all cultures.

- Her success was aided by the increased interest in the relationship between religion and politics in Islamic societies following September 11, 2001* and particularly after the Arab Spring.*

- This success did have its limits, mostly due to her ethnographic* methods (that is, her methods of conducting research in the field and writing up her findings) and because her study took place mostly within mosques.

Assessing The Argument

The driving force in *Politics of Piety:The Islamic Revival and the Feminist Subject* is Saba Mahmood's inquiry into how women's participation in an Islamic piety movement* calls into question Western assumptions that feminist goals can be applied universally.

The book is a wide-ranging discussion of freedom and equality, in which Mahmood questions some of the most important assumptions and preoccupations of secular liberalism* and feminist thought. She takes feminist scholars to task for failing to question an idea that has been central to liberal and progressive thought for a long time: whether the desire to be free from subordination is universal.[1] This has proved to be the most influential aspect of Mahmood's analysis.

Mahmood's argument hinges on her understanding of agency*— the ability of a person to act in the world according to his or her will.

> ❝ On the one hand, women are seen to assert their presence in previously male-defined spheres while, on the other hand, the very idioms they use to enter these arenas are grounded in discourses that have historically secured their subordination to male authority. ❞
>
> Saba Mahmood, *Politics of Piety: The Islamic Revival and the Feminist Subject*

She argues that women's agency has been associated too often only with resistance to dominant norms.*

She then effectively turns this idea on its head, suggesting that the ways in which one lives within or *inhabits* norms—upholding and perpetuating them, rather than seeking to resist, undermine, or overthrow them—can also be understood through the language of agency. So agency is not limited to resisting norms but is better understood as the "capacities and skills required to undertake particular kinds of ethical actions."[2] The women of the piety movement develop the capacities and skills required to live as virtuous Muslims by actively living in accordance with Islamic patriarchal* norms.

Achievement in Context

The success of Saba Mahmood's *Politics of Piety* has been enhanced by the subsequent political upheavals in the Middle East. Events in Egypt since its publication, beginning with the uprising in January 2011, have stirred interest in the interplay of politics and the Islamic revival,* and the transformations underway in Egyptian society have lent her study additional poignancy and relevance.

In this context, Mahmood's achievement is to show how the women of the piety movement seek to preserve the virtues, ethical capacities, and forms of reasoning they believe are under threat from the secularization* (that is, the waning of the influence of religion over political, social, and cultural matters) of Egyptian life. Their practical efforts are directed at "instructing Muslims not only in the proper performance of religious duties and acts of worship but, more importantly, familiarizing them with the tradition of interpreting the Koran* and the hadith*"[3] (the principal scriptures of the Islamic faith).

She demonstrates, however, that this instruction is not simply about passing on knowledge of the texts but also interpreting them to develop a practical guide to conduct in daily affairs. The piety movement is the first in Egyptian history to see such a large number of women playing such a central role in the mosque. But this role does not take the form of resistance to the male-dominated traditions of Islamic pedagogy. Instead, the women give religious discourse a popular form that they hope will reach into Egyptian social life, transforming society in the process and making it more religiously devout.

Limitations

The most serious limitations of *Politics of Piety* come from the same source as its strengths: its ethnographic method. For readers who do not have a strong background in anthropology, Mahmood's methodological approach (that is, the means by which she conducts her research and analysis) might be somewhat unfamiliar, relying as she does upon close observation of a small number of women rather than a survey or tightly structured interview techniques.

Her anthropological approach encourages a non-judgmental standpoint—meaning her questions are different from those scholars in other fields might ask. She aims to understand the women's involvement in the piety movement on their own terms rather than to assess the movement's relative merits in order to praise or condemn it.

The problem is that this is only part of the picture. She presents the views of particular Muslim women as representing a different way of being from that of the secular liberal individual. But she does not inquire into the conflicts and complexities that underlie their pious behavior.

In adopting a non-critical stance, Mahmood "repeats and validates the moral norms of her pious interlocutors."[4] So she criticizes secular feminism for failing to take account of religious difference, but fails to examine differences between the women of the piety movement themselves.

The second limitation is that Mahmood had access to her subjects primarily in mosques and did not see how they behaved in other social situations. As a result, despite her intention to describe ethnographically the details of the women's lives, Mahmood can give us only what they say about their everyday lives within the context of the study sessions.

NOTES

1   Saba Mahmood, *Politics of Piety: The Islamic Revival and the Feminist Subject* (Princeton: Princeton University Press, 2005), 10.

2   Mahmood, *Politics of Piety*, 30.

3   Saba Mahmood, "Rehearsed Spontaneity and the Conventionality of Ritual: Disciplines of Salat," in *American Ethnologist* vol. 28, issue 4 (2008): 829.

4   Melinda Cooper, "Orientalism in the Mirror: The Sexual Politics of Anti-Westernism," in *Theory, Culture & Society* vol. 25, no. 6 (2008): 39.

PLACE IN THE AUTHOR'S WORK

KEY POINTS

- The focus of Mahmood's life's work has been the notion of freedom—from the supposed lack of freedom for Muslim women in *Politics of Piety* to her current work on religious freedom.

- *Politics of Piety* was the first book Mahmood wrote as sole author and was the breakthrough text that launched her career.

- It established Mahmood as an important scholar of gender, Islam, and the Middle East.

Positioning

Politics of Piety: The Islamic Revival and the Feminist Subject is Saba Mahmood's first single-authored book. It was based on two years of fieldwork in Cairo (1995–97) conducted for her doctoral thesis at Stanford University. She wrote the book during postdoctoral fellowships at the University of California at Berkeley and Harvard University. The text can therefore be described as an early work. Mahmood had been involved in politics in her native Pakistan and this book reveals her growing dissatisfaction with the explanations that she and her fellow "progressive leftists" relied upon to explain the popular turn to traditional Islamic ways of organizing society.[1]

The questions Mahmood addressed in *Politics of Piety* about the nature of ritual and the gap between non-Western religious viewpoints and mainstream feminist* thinking have remained central to her subsequent work. To date, Mahmood has produced a coherent body of work in which she has developed her interest in the interaction of religion, politics, and gender.

> ❝ The right to religious liberty is often conceived in individualist terms—whether in the First Amendment, the European Convention on Human Rights, or the Universal Declaration of Human Rights. Yet the right to religious liberty has also been imagined in collective terms as the right of a group to practice its traditions freely, without undue intervention or control. This latter conception has been very important to religious minorities in claiming a place of autonomy and freedom from majoritarian norms and state interventions. I am trying to think through how these alternative conceptions of religious liberty stand in tension with each other and the sorts of impasses it produces. ❞
>
> Saba Mahmood, Interview with Nathan Schneider

What sets *Politics of Piety* apart is its challenge to scholars in the secular liberal feminist* tradition to reassess the assumptions that underpin both their analyses and their political commitments. In addition, her interpretation of agency*—the ability to act in the world according to your own will—overturns previous thinking and is particularly novel, laying the foundations for her later interest in notions of freedom. Mahmood believes agency can include how people live within the norms* of a patriarchal* society—rather than being understood only in terms of resistance to these norms and attempts to overturn or undermine them.

Integration

All of Mahmood's work is concerned with the relationship between religion and politics. Since the publication of *Politics of Piety*, she has published articles and taught courses on secularism, and coauthored a book with the anthropologist Talal Asad,* the feminist political theorist Wendy Brown,* and the influential gender theorist Judith Butler* entitled *Is Critique Secular? Blasphemy, Injury, and Free Speech.*[2]

Her most recent articles[3] deal with the way in which inequalities between the first and third worlds have affected religious liberty differently for religious minorities of the Middle East. She also considers how political and legal engagements are bringing about major changes for religious freedom in South Asia, the Middle East, Europe, and the United States.

In particular, Mahmood has discussed the impact of debates about religious freedom and the rights of minority groups in the Middle East on the lives of native Christians there. She focuses particularly on the rights of groups to preserve their religious identity when it might impinge on the freedom of individuals, particularly women.

The move from *Politics of Piety* to a study of religious liberty and minorities shows the range of Mahmood's work. Those interested in the region would find her body of work discussing the relationship between religious faith and politics in the Middle East, with a particular focus on Egypt, a useful read.

One important thread that connects her early work with her most recent writing is the discussion of personal freedom—ranging from freedom in terms of individual autonomy, covered in *Politics of Piety*, to her current work on religious freedom in international law.[4]

Significance

The Politics of Piety remains Mahmood's only single-authored book and has been very important to her career, establishing her as a major force in the anthropology of gender, religion, ethics, and the Middle East. Its reception was largely positive; the book was translated into French in 2009 when Islam and, in particular, the veiling of Muslim women, had become the focus of public debate in France.

Politics of Piety was a response to the radically altered attitudes to Islam and Islamism* in the West after the terrorist attacks on New

York and Washington, DC, of September 11, 2001.* The book laid the groundwork for Mahmood's subsequent work on freedom and minority rights in the Middle East.

She is currently working on her second book, which will focus on religious liberty and non-Muslim minorities in the Middle East and particularly on Egypt. How this new book is received will inevitably affect how *Politics of Piety* is seen in the future as part of a lifetime's research and within the framework of her own evolving interests and concerns.

NOTES

1   Saba Mahmood, *Politics of Piety: The Islamic Revival and the Feminist Subject* (Princeton: Princeton University Press, 2012), xxii.

2   Talal Asad et al. *Is Critique Secular? Blasphemy, Injury, and Free Speech* (Berkeley: University of California Press, 2009).

3   Saba Mahmood, "Religious Freedom, the Minority Question, and Geopolitics in the Middle East," *Comparative Studies in Society and History* 15 (2) (2012): 418–46; and "Sectarian Conflict and Family Law in Egypt," *American Ethnologist* 39 (1) (2012): 54–62.

4   Nathan Schneider, "Interview with Saba Mahmood," accessed August 7, 2015, http://blogs.ssrc.org/tif/2011/08/17/religious-liberty-minorities-and-islam/.

SECTION 3
IMPACT

MODULE 9
THE FIRST RESPONSES

KEY POINTS

- The most important criticisms of Saba Mahmood's *Politics of Piety* are that she too readily dismisses the feminist* goals of freedom and equality. Her vision of the piety movement* is judged as idealized and she presents the women as nonpolitical.

- Mahmood's response is that her intentions have been misunderstood. Her aim is not to judge her informants' participation in the piety movement on the basis of feminist criteria, but to understand how that participation is unavoidably political.

- The most important factor that shapes responses to the book is political change in the Middle East and ongoing discussions about the position of women in Islamic societies.

Criticism

The most prominent criticism of Saba Mahmood's *Politics of Piety: The Islamic Revival and the Feminist Subject* concerns her approach to feminist thinking. Mahmood believes that women who do not appear to resist, subvert, or undermine religious norms* requiring subordination to patriarchal* values still have agency*—they have chosen this role for themselves. Scholars have taken issue with this idea and think that Mahmood cannot simply dismiss the goals of secular liberal, feminist politics for all.

Social anthropologist Sindre Bangstad,* for example, has pointed to the problem of reconciling feminism with Mahmood's perspective which "appears to prioritize the 'preservation of life forms' over

> ❝ If feminism is to mean anything at all, it is extremely difficult to avoid the conclusion that women's entitlement to rights and dignity regardless of religious and ethnic affiliation must be central to its minimal and core definition. ❞
>
> Sindre Bangstad, "Saba Mahmood and Anthropological Feminism After Virtue"

women's rights."[1] By giving equal weight to her subjects' views and those of secular liberal feminists,* he says that Mahmood is generalizing about both sets of women. This has the effect of artificially setting women who uphold patriarchal values against those who seek to overturn them in the name of liberty, freedom, and equality.

A number of critics have suggested that Mahmood overstates the importance of processes of achieving virtue. For example, the social anthropologist Samuli Schielke* accuses Mahmood of presenting an overly idealized and coherent vision of the piety movement. She suggests that Mahmood has replaced one idealized vision (secular liberalism) with another (the piety movement). Schielke also points out that Mahmood fails tell us about women who have struggled and perhaps failed to live up to the standards of piety. Schielke contends that the image we are presented with is "too perfect."[2]

The anthropologist Amira Mittermaier* has argued that Mahmood is too focused on agency and how the women in the movement consciously cultivate virtue. She believes that this obscures other religious factors that rely less on deliberate individual action than on how individuals can be affected by notions of unpredictable divine interventions and the contingencies of life itself. Mittermaier's ethnography describes an Egyptian Sufi community (a community of followers of an unorthodox and mystical branch of Islam) who experience dreams that are divinely inspired or include visitations.[3]

These dreams, says Mittermaier, are relevant precisely because they are believed to originate not from the dreamer but from another source.

Responses

Although Mahmood did not respond directly to the feminist critique of her work, in 2012 she wrote a new preface to *Politics of Piety*, in which she emphasized that it was never her concern to judge her subjects' actions on the basis of their feminist credentials or the potential of their activities to subvert the patriarchal status quo. Her book is not, therefore, primarily about the restoration of agency to Muslim women who had previously been condemned for their docility in the face of patriarchal religious restrictions. Nor does it seek to compare those women with those who resist such norms in the pursuit of freedom and equality.

Rather, her aim was to nurture a means of "thinking about modalities of agency that exceed liberatory projects."[4] In other words, she wanted to examine alternative forms of agency, ones that do not necessarily conform to feminist, left-wing, or secular liberal aims.

Mahmood believes that those who have responded to her text have tended to focus unduly on the question of "who is or is not deemed 'an agent.'"[5] The implication here is that many of her critics rather missed the point of her book, which was to extend the conventional understanding of agency.

Mahmood believes that ethics cannot be studied separately from politics. To understand the members of the piety movement as agents requires a rethinking of politics that takes into account the women's ethical and ritual practices. Mahmood argues that rather than engaging in direct political activism or making political claims, the women of the piety movement give expression to their politics through their ethics. It is through making themselves pious Muslims that these women engage politically with the society around them.

Conflict and Consensus

Politics of Piety invites readers to "rethink, with far more humility than we are accustomed to, what feminist politics really means."[6] It remains a source of lively debate within feminist anthropology and Middle Eastern studies, and in relation to scholarship on religion, Islamism, and ethics. A question still under debate is whether Mahmood's focus on ethics and self-development is anti-political.

In her 2012 preface she confesses that this view puzzles her as she intended to show how participants in the piety movement in Cairo—despite their claimed nonpolitical stance—were inextricably caught up in politics. She argues that the piety movement has transformed how other kinds of political projects—statist, nationalist, secular liberal—can be imagined and executed.

The social anthropologist Paul Anderson*[7] is one author who has responded to Mahmood's discussion of the way that different understandings of practices like veiling constitute distinct ways of relating to society that are unavoidably political.[8] Like Mittermaier, he focuses on what he regards as shortcomings in the way Mahmood places importance on individual ways of being and acting. He is also unconvinced by Mahmood's focus on individuals. He discusses the practice of moral advice and reproof in religious groups[9] and seeks to supplement Mahmood's work with an understanding of how the social groups work within the piety movement.[10]

These responses call for an understanding of Muslim morality in the everyday lives of ordinary citizens across the Middle East that takes more account of social interaction.

NOTES

1 Sindre Bangstad, "Saba Mahmood and Anthropological Feminism After Virtue," *Theory, Culture & Society* vol. 28, no.3 (2011): 42.

2 Samuli Schielke, "Being Good in Ramadan: Ambivalence, Fragmentation, and the Moral Self in the Lives of Young Egyptians," in *Journal of the Royal Anthropological Institute* 15, suppl. 1 (2009): 36.

3 Amira Mittermaier, "Dreams from Elsewhere: Muslim Subjectivities Beyond the Trope of Self-Cultivation," *Journal of the Royal Anthropological Institute* 18, no. 2 (2012): 247–65.

4 Saba Mahmood, *Politics of Piety: The Islamic Revival and the Feminist Subject* (Princeton: Princeton University Press, 2012), x.

5 Mahmood, *Politics of Piety*, xii.

6 Mahmood, *Politics of Piety*, 38.

7 Paul Anderson, "'The Piety of the Gift': Selfhood and Sociality in the Egyptian Mosque Movement," *Anthropological Theory* 11, no. 1 (2011): 3–21.

8 Mahmood, *Politics of Piety*, xii.

9 Anderson, "'The Piety of the Gift'": 4.

10 Anderson, "'The Piety of the Gift'": 20.

MODULE 10
THE EVOLVING DEBATE

KEY POINTS

- The most important impact *Politics of Piety* has made is its contribution to the "ethical turn"* in anthropology in which ethics, previously a matter for philosophy, became central to the discipline.

- It should be considered alongside the work of a number of anthropologists who have applied Foucault's insights about ethical self-formation* (virtuous self-improvement) in their ethnographic* studies.

- The impact of this approach has been a shift in anthropological thinking. Instead of analyzing the meaning of symbols and the sociological function of religion, there is a new focus on understanding everyday religious practices and how the individual experiences ethical behavior rather than the way such behavior can be imposed.

Uses And Problems

In *Politics of Piety: The Islamic Revival and the Feminist Subject* Saba Mahmood is not principally concerned with the meaning of religious practices, but rather with the ways in which people use such practices to produce virtuous selves. This approach was pioneered by her mentor, the anthropologist Talal Asad,* whose 1993 book *Genealogies of Religion: Discipline and Reasons of Power in Christianity and Islam*[1] insisted on the importance of physical discipline in medieval ascetic practices and how these practices formed the true Christian.

Asad is well known for arguing against the mainstream symbolic understanding of religion dominant in the 1980s. Although Mahmood's work has been criticized for sidelining symbolic

> **❝** The monastic program that prescribes the performance of rites is directed at forming and reforming Christian dispositions. The most important of these is the will to obey what is seen as the truth, and therefore the guardians of that truth. The achievement of that disposition is the Christian virtue of humility. **❞**
>
> Talal Asad, *Genealogies of Religion: Discipline and Reasons of Power in Christianity and Islam*

significance, its strength is that, like Asad's, it calls attention instead to everyday ethical life.

Besides Mahmood, this approach—inspired by the French social theorist Michel Foucault's* late writings—has been developed by the anthropologists Veena Das* and Michael Lambek.* Das's study *Life and Words: Violence and the Descent into the Ordinary* pays close attention to the way that ethical ideas are woven into the dense fabric of everyday life in India.[2] Michael Lambek has developed similar inquiries into ethics in everyday life in Madagascar, and his edited collection *Ordinary Ethics: Anthropology, Language, and Action*[3] most clearly illustrates how he shares Mahmood's approach.

Mahmood's husband, the anthropologist Charles Hirschkind,* is a clear intellectual ally. Hirschkind's work also relates to the Islamic revival* in Egypt and shares many of Mahmood's beliefs and concerns. His 2006 book *The Ethical Soundscape: Cassette Sermons and Islamic Counterpublics*[4] has been highly influential among anthropologists and scholars of the Middle East, in particular. Hirschkind's study is complementary to Mahmood's and focuses on male members of the Egyptian piety movement,* including preachers and preaching instructors and the men who listen to and discuss their sermons through recorded media.

Together, Mahmood and Hirschkind have made a significant

contribution to understanding the broader Islamic revival in the Middle East. Their work is perhaps best seen alongside that of Asad, Lambek and Das in advocating an approach to religion and morality that focuses on processes of ethical self-formation rather than rules.

According to this new thinking, human beings are free ethical subjects even when they appear to follow a moral code imposed by their group or religion. Conformity itself is an ethical choice.

Schools of Thought

Politics of Piety contributed to a contemporary surge of interest in ethics and morality within anthropology. The text entered the debate about the ethnographic applications of Foucault's work on ethics and it continues to inspire scholars to reflect on how this approach fits within the broad fields of feminist* anthropology and the anthropology of religion.

In his recent book, *The Subject of Virtue: An Anthropology of Ethics and Freedom*[5] the social anthropologist James Laidlaw* discusses virtue and freedom. Like Mahmood, he draws on Aristotle's* virtue ethics,* arguing that virtues do not depend on imposed rules and norms but on engagement in particular practices. He supports Mahmood's argument that debate about agency too often simply reflects the view of the debaters—usually that agency requires openly manifested resistance.[6]

In his *An Anthropology of Ethics*,[7] James Faubion,* professor of anthropology at Rice University in Texas, shares Mahmood's admiration for Foucault* and the processes of ethical self-formation. He goes on to argue for examining interactions with "ethical others"[8] to understand how the moral order changes over time.

Faubion has an original approach to ethics, arguing that Foucault's framework is in need of revision if it is to work for ethnographic anthropology. It must, he thinks, embrace the diversity of ethical practices that Mahmood highlights, as well as resolving the related problem of relativism.*

For authors like Faubion, Lambek, and Laidlaw, all forms of ethical practice require freedom. The questions Mahmood raises in *Politics of Piety* about the nature and limits of freedom in relation to ethical practices continue to play a major role in the debate.

In Current Scholarship

Political actions, commitments, and aspirations are still under the spotlight in Egypt. The revolutionary uprising in January 2011, which resulted in the overthrow of the elected government and a change in leadership from President Hosni Mubarak* to Mohammed Morsi,* was followed by Morsi's subsequent deposition. Upheaval continues in Egypt, with Islamist* movements taking center stage and lending Mahmood's study additional relevance.

The question of politics in Mahmood's work is ripe for revisiting, particularly as some scholars have regarded her approach as anti-political. For others, *Politics of Piety* has provided a jumping-off point both for new theories and ethnographic explorations of ethics and everyday life.

The ethical turn in anthropology has brought together several traditions of inquiry. The resulting approach focuses on moral behavior being examined on its own terms.

This entails a shift from seeing morality as collective, as argued by the pioneering French sociologist Emile Durkheim,* to a focus on the subjective ethical view of the individual. It is a shift from focusing on how ethical behavior is imposed to how it is experienced.

Michael Lambek suggests in his book *Ordinary Ethics* that ethical questions have traditionally been bound up with questions about religion[9] and this has disguised how individuals learn to live with them. Mahmood's exploration of how the religious life can justify, instill, and resist moral norms has been crucial to the development of this argument.

NOTES

1   Talal Asad, *Genealogies of Religion: Discipline and Reasons of Power in Christianity and Islam* (Baltimore: Johns Hopkins University Press, 1993).

2   Veena Das, *Life and Words: Violence and the Descent into the Ordinary* (Berkeley: University of California Press, 2006).

3   Michael Lambek, ed., *Ordinary Ethics: Anthropology, Language, and Action* (New York: Fordham University Press, 2010).

4   Charles Hirschkind, *The Ethical Soundscape: Cassette Sermons and Islamic Counterpublics* (New York: Columbia University Press, 2006).

5   James Laidlaw, *The Subject of Virtue: An Anthropology of Ethics and Freedom* (Cambridge: Cambridge University Press, 2014).

6   James Laidlaw, *The Subject of Virtue*, 6.

7   James Faubion, *An Anthropology of Ethics* (Cambridge: Cambridge University Press 2011).

8   Faubion, *An Anthropology of Ethics*, 120.

9   Lambek, *Ordinary Ethics*, 3.

IMPACT AND INFLUENCE TODAY

KEY POINTS

- *Politics of Piety* remains a source of debate about the nature of agency,* ethics, and freedom as well as the relationship between religion, politics, and everyday life.

- Mahmood portrays the members of the women's piety movement* as individuals engaged in ethical self-formation* rather than as victims or deluded fundamentalists. This view still challenges scholars to rethink their ideas about freedom and equality and the possibility that submission to external authority can be regarded as a condition of self-fulfillment.

- There has been a range of responses to this challenge. One is to restate the feminist* commitment to universal ideals of freedom and equality. Another is to question the significance of the differences it highlights between practices of ethical self-formation and secular liberal* ideas about ethics.

Position

Given that Saba Mahmood's *Politics of Piety: The Islamic Revival and the Feminist Subject* is a recent publication and that, at the time of writing, it is only eight years since it first appeared, it is difficult and not particularly useful to distinguish between current and earlier reactions to the book.

The text remains a source of lively debate within feminist anthropology and Middle Eastern studies, and in relation to scholarship on religion, the Islamic revival* and ethics. It remains an important challenge to secular liberal feminist scholars. This challenge has met

> ❝ The domains of religion and politics are not easily kept separate for analytical purposes ... Ideas expressed in and actions taken within apparently different domains and institutions feed into each other, and what belongs to the public sphere or the private sphere is to be investigated and not assumed. ❞
>
> Harri Englund, *Christianity and Public Culture In Africa*

with mixed responses, as Mahmood herself admits in the 2012 preface to the paperback edition.

Some feminists praised the book for what they saw as the restoration of agency to Muslim women in the piety movement who had previously been regarded as docile in the face of patriarchal* religious restrictions. Others responded less positively, in particular about how Mahmood puts on an equal footing women who work towards feminist goals of freedom and equality, and those who abide by Islamic virtues such as female modesty, thereby reinforcing patriarchal norms.*

Mahmood is dismissive of both readings of her work. Neither, she believes, recognizes that her intention was not to pass judgment. She does not seek to heap praise or denigration on the Cairo women, by appraising either their feminist credentials or the subversive potential of their activities.[1] Instead, her aim was to rethink the meaning of freedom and agency from the perspective of female participants in the Islamic revival.

This is just as relevant today when Islamist* militancy is considered a serious threat by many Western liberal nations and is often symbolized by images of veiled Muslim women. The media stereotype of the "Jihadi bride"*[2]—women who leave their lives in the West to marry men fighting on behalf of militant Islamic groups—is rarely accompanied by any analysis of why young western Muslim women might want to go to join a movement generally regarded as terrible in its treatment of women. *Politics of Piety* is an important source of information for anyone working on this subject.

Interaction

Mahmood is one of a group of writers inspired by the French philosopher Michel Foucault* and ultimately by the Aristotelian tradition of virtue ethics* (an approach to ethics that emphasizes the capacity afforded us by our character to behave in a virtuous fashion).

Politics of Piety has been influential in bringing religious commitment, morality, and ethical self-formation* to the fore in the study of Islamic societies in the Middle East. More broadly, it has inspired scholars working in the fields of the anthropology of ethics and morality, regardless of region. This can be seen in the work of scholars such as Paul Anderson* and Michael Lambek* who have both engaged with Mahmood's text and built on her analyses.

Michael Lambek, for example, argues that exploring the complex textures of everyday ethical practices can "shift or deepen our understanding of social life more generally."[3] Such scholarship takes as a starting point dissatisfaction with earlier work in this field, characterized by the philosopher Kant's* deontological* understanding of ethics and the work of the French sociologist Emile Durkheim.*

For Lambek and his fellow-supporters of the ethical turn* in anthropology, these viewpoints are concerned too much with society's upholding of moral rules and too little with the personal processes of deliberation and decision-making. As Lambek argues, moral and ethical questions have historically centered on religion as the means by which "the ordinary is transcended and ethics intellectualized, materialized, or transcendentalized."[4] By this he means that in the past religion has been the only domain in which ethical behavior is defined.

So to behave ethically is to do one's duty as defined in this religious domain, irrespective of one's state of mind. By showing how working ethically on yourself can justify, instill, and resist moral norms,* Mahmood provides an alternative approach to the relationship between religion, morality, and ethics.

The Continuing Debate

Politics of Piety is very much part of an active scholarly debate today. Indeed, given it was published only in 2005, that debate can still be described as young, lively, and immediate.

Debates surrounding the text cross traditional academic boundaries, incorporating voices from anthropology, religious studies, Middle Eastern studies, and gender studies. All of these responses, however, have not really united into organized schools of thought at particular institutions. Nor can they be described as enjoying the coordinated "leadership" of particular individuals.

Mahmood is often grouped among advocates of the ethical turn in anthropology inspired by the work of Michel Foucault, according to which ethics, previously a concern of philosophers, became greatly more important to anthropologists.

Anthropologists such as Harri Englund* have challenged the implied rejection of earlier anthropological work that draws on Durkheim's ideas. He sees, particularly in the early anthropology of central and southern Africa (notably that of the South African anthropologist Max Gluckman)* a more subtle approach to morality. Englund maintains that this earlier anthropology of morality has much to recommend it, particularly when it comes to understanding the importance of society, obligations, and interdependency in the field of moral reasoning rather than a purely individual focus.

NOTES

1 Saba Mahmood, *Politics of Piety: The Islamic Revival and the Feminist Subject* (Princeton: Princeton University Press, 2012), x.

2 See, for example, "'Jihadi bride' Aqsa Mahmood denies recruiting London girls," BBC News, March 16, 2015, accessed July 11, 2015, http://www.bbc.co.uk/news/uk-31913429.

3 Michael Lambek, "Introduction" in *Ordinary Ethics: Anthropology, Language, and Action,* ed. Michael Lambek (New York: Fordham University Press, 2010), 7.

4 Lambek, *Ordinary Ethics*, 3.

WHERE NEXT?

KEY POINTS

- *Politics of Piety* is likely to remain important in understanding political and social events in Egypt in the wake of the popular uprising there in 2011.

- The text will continue to have an impact since it provides a rich source of ethnographic* detail about the ethical and religious practices of a group of Muslim women.

- The challenges it makes to the assumptions of secular feminism* and Western liberalism* make this a seminal text.

Potential

Since Saba Mahmood published *Politics of Piety: The Islamic Revival and the Feminist Subject*, events in Egypt, beginning with the uprising in January 2011 and continuing through to the time of writing, have generated interest in a central theme of the book—the interplay of politics and Islamism* (a movement founded on the belief that Islam provides the best model for government and society).

These upheavals create new debates, unanticipated by Mahmood when she was writing, which she will no doubt enter. She has, in fact, addressed these debates in the preface to the 2012 paperback issue.

There she explains how by 2008, when she returned to Cairo to carry out fieldwork, she noticed that the distinctions between secularists* (those who would prefer less religious influence in civic life) and Islamists* had become less sharp. Egyptians seemed to be uniting across former divisions in the light of increasing poverty, deteriorating public services, and the violent excesses of the security police.

> **❝** Her writings represent in many ways a challenge to the ways 'Western' secular feminism has chosen to conceptualize gender issues in the so-called 'Muslim world'. In pointing out how many of these conceptualizations have reflected the categories of many academics aligned to such traditions of thought themselves, Mahmood has made an important anthropological intervention. This comes at a point in time when the need for a re-thinking of categories of thought is more important than ever for a feminist and anthropological engagement with 'the lives of others'. **❞**
>
> Sindre Bangstadt, *Saba Mahmood and Anthropological Feminism After Virtue*

Mahmood found that many women in the piety movement,* who had previously avoided direct political confrontation with the state, now participated in protests and had no concerns about the compatibility of their commitment to Islamic piety with voicing demands for political and civic freedom. She suggests that this rather undermines early forecasts that the Egyptian uprising was the beginning of a "post-Islamist" era.[1]

Egypt's current situation is complex and it is difficult to identify the beginnings of future developments and the roots of those in the recent past. This suggests that Mahmood's text will remain relevant as readers turn to it with changing questions. Given her challenges to generalizations about Islam and gender politics, her future publications will be eagerly awaited by scholars in anthropology, politics, gender, and religious studies.

Future Directions

Mahmood's recent work is driven by her belief that human rights are best protected by understanding which issues are really being disputed in struggles concerning religious freedom. The revolutionary uprisings in Egypt and across much of North Africa and the Middle East, once referred to as the Arab Spring,* have both increased the relevance of *Politics of Piety* and opened up new questions.

The right to religious liberty is often conceived as an individual's right to choose what religion he or she professes. Religious liberty is also understood in terms of a group's right to follow its traditions without constraint. In her most recent work, Mahmood is grappling with the tension between these different conceptions of religious liberty and the sorts of impasses it produces. Ultimately, she questions whether either of these interpretations of religious freedom is helpful in resolving this situation.

Mahmood's work is an important contribution to the increasingly significant study of contemporary religious groups, sometimes known as "fundamentalists," in the Middle East and other places. Members of these groups do not accept the contemporary secular liberal model of politics and civic society and *Politics of Piety* highlights how they are often, therefore, referred to as "medieval." As Judith Butler* has noted, modernity is often associated with gender equality and sexual freedom.[2] People in religious groups are set apart in this conception of modernity, on the grounds that they submit—or are perceived to submit—to different arrangements in sexual politics and relations between the genders.

Summary

Politics of Piety was published after the terrorist attacks of September 11, 2001* amid a climate of fear surrounding Islam in the popular press. Representations of Islam and the status of Muslim women were remarkably, even dangerously, limited and superficial.

This context, which included the military intervention in the Middle East by the United States and its allies known as the "War on

Terror,"* gave the book particular significance.

Since then, revolutionary uprisings across the Middle East, including in Egypt, have shifted the terrain on which the book stands, both enhancing its relevance and altering the kinds of questions that readers are likely to bring to it. The entanglement of ethics, religion, and politics so central to Mahmood's study is a core concern of scholars and other observers seeking to understand the events in Egypt and across the Middle East and North Africa, both in terms of the dramatic transformations of the recent past and what the future holds.

Although it is impossible to assess the long-term influence of *Politics of Piety* only eight years on from its original publication, it is certainly has the makings of a classic study. Mahmood has made an important intellectual contribution by identifying mainstream secular feminist views as central to the exclusion of practicing Muslims today. For that reason alone, *Politics of Piety* is likely to be essential reading for many years to come for undergraduate anthropology students.

NOTES

1   Saba Mahmood, *Politics of Piety: The Islamic Revival and the Feminist Subject* (Princeton: Princeton University Press, 2012), xviii.

2   Judith Butler, *Frames of War: When Is Life Grievable?* (London: Verso 2009), 105.

GLOSSARY

GLOSSARY OF TERMS

Agency: in academic use, "agency" implies the ability of a person (sometimes referred to as an "agent") to act in the world. Mahmood argues that agency has been too readily associated with resistance, and she seeks to modify its meaning to account for the ways in which individuals inhabit norms, thereby serving to uphold rather than directly challenge the status quo.

Al Qaeda: a global militant Islamist organization founded by the militant leader Osama bin Laden. It operates as a network and comprises both a multinational, stateless army and an Islamist, extremist, jihadist group.

Arab Spring: a term used in the media to describe a series of violent and nonviolent protests, demonstrations, and civil wars that swept through the Arab world starting on December 18, 2010. As a result of the Arab Spring, rulers have been forced from power in Tunisia, Egypt, Libya, and Yemen, and civil wars have erupted and are continuing in Bahrain and Syria.

Autonomy: an individual's freedom to make an informed decision that is not subject to external control. Political and moral philosophy often determines whether people can make autonomous decisions when judging the extent to which they are morally responsible and accountable for what they do.

Collective unconscious: elements of the unconscious mind shared by all humans; the concept and term were proposed by Swiss psychologist Carl Jung.

Communitarianism: a philosophy that stresses the relationship between community and individual.

Cultural anthropology: a term used in the United States for the study of human cultures and societies.

Deontological: an understanding of ethics inspired by German philosopher Immanuel Kant, for whom ethics was a matter of rationality, independent of social context. Kant argued that an action could only be ethical if it was a product of reason not a result of habituated virtue.

Embodiment: the experience of being physically present in the world.

Ethical subject: a thinking individual capable of making moral decisions.

Ethical self-formation: the process by which individuals constitute themselves as ethical subjects.

Ethical turn: a movement in anthropology in which matters relating to ethics, previously a concern for the field of philosophy, became central to the discipline.

Ethnography: a research methodology and writing style central to the discipline of anthropology, pioneered by the early anthropologists Bronislaw Malinowski in the UK and Franz Boas in the US. It relies upon intensive fieldwork and observation of participants intended to produce a deep understanding of the context in which the lives of those under study unfold.

Feminism: a political position arguing for the equal treatment of women and men. Feminist social science goes further, offering a critique of male bias in the production of knowledge about the world. Feminist anthropology takes as its premise the idea that the study of women's beliefs and practices is critical to understanding human social life.

First and third worlds: traditional labels for the developed, industrialized countries (principally in North America, Europe, Australia, and Japan) and the developing, less industrialized countries (principally in Latin America, Asia, and Africa). The concept of the first world was introduced during the Cold War to distinguish the capitalist West (the United States, Western Europe and Japan) from the "second world" of the communist East (the Soviet Union and allies); the "third world" was the label given to developing countries.

First Gulf War: a US-led military campaign involving troops from 34 nations, fought in 1990–91 to counter Iraq's invasion of Kuwait.

Gender studies: a field of academic inquiry focused on female/male identities and cultural representations.

Hadith: an Arabic term for "narrative" or "report," usually referring to a record of the words and deeds of the Prophet, his family and companions. In common usage, the term refers to the entire collection of the Prophet's actions and speech.

Ideal virtuous self: the model of good ethical behavior aspired to by members of a particular cultural group.

Iranian Revolution: also known as the Islamic Revolution, a revolt in Iran that swept the US-backed Mohammad Reza Shah Pahlavi from power and led to the establishment of an Islamic republic led by Grand Ayatollah Ruhollah Khomeini.

ISIL: acronym for the Islamic State of Iraq and the Levant, a militant group active in the civil war that began in Syria in 2011, and which on June 29, 2014, declared itself a worldwide caliphate (global government).

Islamism: a set of ideologies holding that the teachings of Islam should guide social and political as well as personal life. Islamist movements tend to aim at the development of an Islamic state and the imposition of Islamic law.

Islamic revival: Mahmood defines "Islamic revival" as "a term that refers not only to the activities of state-oriented political groups but more broadly to a religious ethos or sensibility that has developed within contemporary Muslim societies" (*Politics of Piety: The Islamic Revival and the Feminist Subject*).

Jihadi bride: a term used by the Western media to refer to Muslim women who leave their homes in the West to travel to the Middle East to join Islamist groups engaged in conflict there.

The Koran (also Qur'an or Quran): the primary Islamic religious text, believed by Muslims to have been revealed by Allah (God) to the Prophet Muhammad over the course of 23 years from 609 onwards.

Late Liberalism Project: a forum for the discussion of liberalism's wide-ranging forms. Key participants include Lauren Berlant (professor of English, University of Chicago) and Elizabeth Povinelli (professor of Anthropology and Gender Studies, Columbia University). Most notably they have sought to produce a critical theory of the complex ideas characteristic of contemporary Western civilization that they call "late liberalism," by carefully describing the practices and ideas of a variety social movements.

Liberalism: a political philosophy that has profoundly influenced Western society. Liberalism emphasizes ideas about individual freedom and equality. Liberals espouse a wide array of views, supporting free speech, a free press, free self-expression in religion, the unregulated operation of capitalist markets, democratic government, and civil rights for members of a society.

Marxism: both a method of societal analysis that focuses on class relations and societal conflict, and a theory that claims historical change occurs through class conflict and transformations in the economic means of production.

Norms: expected, agreed, or prescribed forms of behavior in a given context.

Patriarchal: pertaining to a social system in which seniority, in both private and public life, is reserved for men.

Piety Movement: a cultural shift in which women from diverse social backgrounds joined together to help one another in a more formalized Islamic study, focusing not only on scripture but also on how to conduct themselves in a virtuous way in contemporary society.

Postcolonialism (also Postcolonial Studies, Postcolonial Theory): the academic study of the cultural legacy left by imperialism and colonialism.

Relativism: the argument that no judgment—of moral or aesthetic value, say—can be said to have an absolute truth; all have relative value depending on subjective point-of-view.

Secularization: a society's shift from reliance on religious institutions and values to secular ones, referring in particular to the separation of politics and religion.

Secularism: the principle of the separation of religion from the state. A secular state is considered to be neutral on matters of belief, and does not impose religion or religious practices upon its people.

Secular liberal feminism: liberalism is a political philosophy founded on ideas about individual freedom and equality. Secular liberalism is associated with the separation of religion from politics. Secular liberal feminism upholds these values in relation to the freedom and equality of individual women.

Secular nationalism: nationalism is a belief or political ideology that involves an individual identifying with, or becoming attached to, his or her nation. Secular nationalism asserts that the nation is not defined by any particular religion and that national identities are more important than religious ones.

September 11, 2001 or 9/11: on this date four coordinated terror attacks were launched against America by the Islamic extremist group Al Qaeda. Four passenger airplanes were flown into various targets around the country, including the World Trade Center in New York City and the Pentagon. The death toll of 2,977 civilians made it the largest attack against America in modern history.

Sharia law: the Islamic legal system derived from the religious precepts of Islam, particularly the Koran and the Hadith. Sharia law governs private as well as public beliefs and behavior—in contrast to many other legal codes, which principally regulate behavior in the public sphere.

Thick description: a method popularized in anthropology by the anthropologist Clifford Geertz in his best-known book, *The Interpretation of Cultures* (1973). The idea is that anthropologists should describe in as much detail as possible the events and interactions they study in order to enable interpretation. It relies on the premise that, through the thick description of the context in which events unfold, unfamiliar cultural practices will become intelligible to outsiders.

Virtue ethics: an approach to ethics usually traced back to Aristotle, which emphasizes the role of character and the virtues it embodies for determining or evaluating ethical behavior.

War on Terror: an international military campaign led by the United States and launched in the wake of the terrorist attacks of September 11, 2001 on the US. President George W. Bush first characterized the campaign as a "war on terror" on September 20, 2001, and the phrase entered common usage. The wars in Afghanistan (from 2001) and Iraq (from 2003) were part of the war on terror.

PEOPLE MENTIONED IN THE TEXT

Lila Abu-Lughod (b. 1952) is an anthropologist and professor of social science at Columbia University. Her research focuses on the relationship between cultural forms and power, the politics of knowledge and representation, and women's rights in the Middle East. Her works include *Writing Women's Worlds: Bedouin Stories* and *Dramas of Nationhood: The Politics of Television in Egypt*.

Aristotle (384–322 B.C.E.) was a philosopher in ancient Greece. He is widely considered to be one of the founders of Western philosophy. His work on ethics, in which he emphasizes the importance of external bodily practices to the cultivation of inward dispositions, continues to inspire scholars to this day.

Paul Anderson is the Prince Alwaleed Lecturer in the department of Middle Eastern Studies at the University of Cambridge, the assistant director of the University's Prince Alwaleed Centre of Islamic Studies, and a fellow of Darwin College, Cambridge. Dr. Anderson is a social anthropologist who focuses on politics, language, morality, and value in the Arab world. His work includes discussion of the political and social effects of speech in Egypt and Syria.

Talal Asad (b. 1933) is an anthropologist based at the City University of New York Graduate Center. He has written extensively on postcolonialism, Islam, and Christianity. Probably his most influential work within anthropology is *Anthropology and the Colonial Encounter*, but key texts relating to the issues raised in Saba Mahmood's work include his 1986 text *The Idea of an Anthropology of Islam, Occasional Papers Series* and his more recent books *Genealogies of Religion: Discipline and Reasons of Power in Christianity and Islam* and *Formations of the Secular: Christianity, Islam, Modernity*.

Sindre Bangstad (b. 1973) is a social anthropologist with research experience on Muslims in South Africa and Norway. He is a postdoctoral fellow at the department of social anthropology at the University of Oslo in Norway and is currently writing a book on new Muslim public intellectuals in Norway.

Janice Boddy (b. 1951) is a Canadian anthropologist. She is currently professor of anthropology at the University of Toronto. Her interests include medical anthropology, religion, gender, and colonialism in Sudan and the Middle East. Her works include *Wombs and Alien Spirits: Women, Men, and the Zar Cult in Northern Sudan*; *Aman: The Story of a Somali Girl* (with Virginia Lee Barnes); and *Civilizing Women: British Crusades in Colonial Sudan*.

Wendy Brown (b. 1955) is professor of political science at the University of California at Berkeley. Much of her work has focused on theories of modern power, and she is highly regarded for her contributions to feminist theory.

Judith Butler (b. 1956) is an American philosopher known for her contributions to feminist and queer theory. She teaches in the rhetoric and comparative literature departments at the University of California at Berkeley, and is also Hannah Arendt Professor of Philosophy at the European Graduate School. She is the author of several books; in particular, *Gender Trouble: Feminism and the Subversion of Identity* is a modern classic.

Veena Das (b. 1945) is Krieger-Eisenhower Professor of Anthropology at the Johns Hopkins University. She also serves on the executive board of the Institute of Socio-Economic Research on Development and Democracy in India. She has published extensively as an ethnographer of India. Beyond India, her research has contributed to the anthropology of violence, suffering, and the State.

Emile Durkheim (1858–1917) was a French sociologist and is considered one of the founding fathers of the discipline of sociology. His *The Elementary Forms of Religious Life*, first published in 1912, influenced twentieth-century anthropologists in their work on questions of ethics and morality.

Harri Englund (b. 1966) is a professor in social anthropology at Churchill College, Cambridge University. He has conducted ethnographic fieldwork in southern and east Africa, primarily in Malawi but also in Mozambique and Zambia. His research interests range from the anthropology of law, human rights, and morality to the study of religion and popular culture.

James Faubion (b. 1957) is a professor of anthropology at Rice University in Texas. He is best known for his work on ethics, but his interests include kinship, social and cultural theory, aesthetics, heterodoxy, and radicalism. He is the author of *An Anthropology of Ethics* and two edited volumes of *Essential Works of Michel Foucault*.

Michel Foucault (1926–84) was a French philosopher renowned for his theorization of power. In contemporary anthropology, his work has also contributed to a recent turn to ethics as an area of inquiry, and, here, scholars take their inspiration largely from Foucault's *The History of Sexuality, Vol. 2: The Use of Pleasure*, translated by Robert Hurley.

Max Gluckman (1911–75) was a South African anthropologist who is remembered as the founder of the Manchester School of Social Anthropology. In his books *Judicial Process Among the Barotse of Northern Rhodesia* and *The Ideas in Barotse Jurisprudence* he explored questions of morality and obligation in ways that have perhaps gone largely unappreciated by scholars writing about ethics today, including Mahmood.

Charles Hirschkind is an anthropologist based at the University of California at Berkeley. His book *The Ethical Soundscape: Cassette Sermons and Islamic Counterpublics* has been highly influential among anthropologists and scholars of the Middle East, in particular. Like Mahmood's study, Hirschkind's work relates to the Islamic revival in Egypt.

Samuel Huntington (1927–2008) was an American academic and political scientist. A professor at Harvard University and director of Harvard's Center for International Affairs, he served during the administration of US President Jimmy Carter as coordinator of security planning for the National Security Council. He is known above all for his 1993 theory, "The Clash of Civilizations," which argued that in the era after the Cold War the religious and cultural identity of different groups would become the principle source of conflict.

Carl Jung (1875–1961) was a Swiss psychologist whose theories about the human personality are particularly significant in the study of religion and culture. He developed the idea of the collective unconscious and of archetypes (mental images in the unconscious mind common to all people).

Immanuel Kant (1724–1804) was a German philosopher whose work is central to modern European philosophy. In Kant's view, ethics and reason are closely related. His major works relating to ethics include the *Critique of Practical Reason* (Kritik der praktischen Vernunft, 1788) and *The Metaphysics of Morals* (Die Metaphysik der Sitten, 1797).

James Laidlaw is head of the division of social anthropology at King's College, Cambridge University. He has investigated the interaction between ethical and anthropological theory, and between ritual and religion.

Michael Lambek is professor of anthropology at the University of Toronto. Religion and ethics are his major research focus and his edited book *Ordinary Ethics: Anthropology, Language, and Action* most clearly illustrates his affinity with Mahmood's approach.

Karl Marx (1818–83) was a German political philosopher and economist whose analysis of class relations under capitalism and articulation of a more egalitarian system provided the basis for communism. Together with Friedrich Engels, Marx wrote *The Communist Manifesto* (1848); he articulated his full theory of production and class relations in *Das Kapital* (1867–94).

Amira Mittermaier (b. 1974) is an anthropologist by training and works at the University of Toronto in the Department for the Study of Religion and the Department of Near and Middle Eastern Civilization. Her research focuses on modern Islam in Egypt.

Mohammed Morsi (b. 1951) is an Egyptian politician, who was fifth president of Egypt from June 30, 2012, to July 3, 2013, when the country's armed forces removed him from office. He was Egypt's first democratically elected president.

Hosni Mubarak (b. 1928) was the fourth president of Egypt from 1981 to 2011. He resigned from power in the 2011 Egyptian revolution.

Samuli Schielke (b. 1972) is a social anthropologist working at the Zentrum Moderner Orient in Berlin. His research focuses on everyday religiosity and morality, aspiration, and frustration. Much of his work concerns the Islamic revival in Egypt.

Stanley Jeragaya Tambiah (1929–2014) was a social anthropologist who investigated the anthropology of politics and religion and made studies of Sri Lanka, Thailand, and the Tamils. He was emeritus professor of anthropology at Harvard University.

Charles Taylor (b. 1931) is a Canadian philosopher associated with the communitarian critique of liberal notions of the self, which seeks to restore a focus on the social institutions and social contexts in which lives are lived and become meaningful. Key publications in this regard include his 1985 articles "Atomism," in *Philosophy and the Human Sciences Philosophical Papers 2* and "What's Wrong with Negative Liberty?" in *Philosophy and the Human Sciences*.

Victor Turner (1920–1983) was a British cultural anthropologist, a notable member of the Manchester School of Social Anthropology. He particularly studied rites of passage, rituals, and symbol and focused on the Ndembu tribe of Zambia; his field is often labeled symbolic and interpretive anthropology.

Muhammad Zia-ul-Haq (1924–88) was Chief of Army Staff in Pakistan who deposed Prime Minister Zulkifar Ali Bhutto and declared martial law in 1977, becoming the country's sixth president. He was in power from 1977 to 1988.

WORKS CITED

WORKS CITED

Abu-Lughod, Lila. *Veiled Sentiments: Honor and Poetry in a Bedouin Society*. Berkeley: University of California Press, 1986.

____. "The Romance of Resistance: Tracing Transformations of Power Through Bedouin Women." *American Ethnologist* 17, no. 1 (1990): 41–55.

Anderson, Paul. "'The Piety of the Gift': Selfhood and Sociality in the Egyptian Mosque Movement." *Anthropological Theory* vol. 11, no. 1 (2011): 3–21.

Asad, Talal. *Formations of the Secular: Christianity, Islam, Modernity*. Stanford: Stanford University Press, 2003.

____. *Genealogies of Religion: Discipline and Reasons of Power in Christianity and Islam*. Baltimore: Johns Hopkins University Press, 1993.

____. *The Idea of an Anthropology of Islam*. Occasional Papers Series. Washington, D.C.: Center for Contemporary Arab Studies, Georgetown University, 1986.

Asad, Talal, Wendy Brown, Judith Butler, and Saba Mahmood. *Is Critique Secular? Blasphemy, Injury, and Free Speech*. Berkeley: University of California Press, 2009.

Bangstad, Sindre. "Saba Mahmood and Anthropological Feminism After Virtue." *Culture & Society* vol. 28, no. 3 (2011): 28–54.

Bell, Catherine. *Ritual Theory, Ritual Practice*. Oxford: Oxford University Press, 1992.

Boddy, Janice. *Civilizing Women: British Crusades in Colonial Sudan*. Princeton: Princeton University Press, 2007.

____. *Wombs and Alien Spirits: Women, Men, and the Zar Cult in Northern Sudan*. Madison: University of Wisconsin Press, 1989.

Boddy, Janice and Virginia Lee Barnes. *Aman: The Story of a Somali Girl*. New York: Vintage Books, 1994.

Butler, Judith. *Frames of War: When Is Life Grievable?* London: Verso 2009.

____. *Gender Trouble: Feminism and the Subversion of Identity*. London: Routledge, 1989.

Cooper, Melinda. "Orientalism in the Mirror: The Sexual Politics of Anti-Westernism." In *Theory, Culture & Society* vol. 25, no. 6 (2008): 25–49.

Das, Veena. *Life and Words: Violence and the Descent into the Ordinary*. Berkeley: University of California Press, 2006.

Durkheim, Emile. *The Elementary Forms of Religious Life*. Translated by Joseph Ward Swain. London: Allen and Unwin, 1976.

Englund, Harri, ed. *Christianity and Public Culture In Africa*. Athens: Ohio University Press, 2012.

Fassin, Didier. "The Ethical Turn in Anthropology: Promises and Uncertainties." *Hau: Journal of Ethnographic Theory* vol. 4, no. 1 (2014): 429–35.

Faubion, James. *An Anthropology of Ethics*. Cambridge: Cambridge University Press, 2011.

Foucault, Michel. *The History of Sexuality, Vol. 2: The Use of Pleasure*. Translated by Robert Hurley. London: Penguin Books, 1985.

Gluckman, Max. *The Ideas in Barotse Jurisprudence.* New Haven: Yale University Press, 1965.

___. *Judicial Process Among the Barotse of Northern Rhodesia*. Manchester: Manchester University Press, 1955.

Hirschkind, Charles. *The Ethical Soundscape: Cassette Sermons and Islamic Counterpublics*. New York: Columbia University Press, 2006.

Huntington, Samuel. *The Clash of Civilizations and the Remaking of World Order.* London: Simon and Schuster, 2002.

Kant, Immanuel. *Critique of Practical Reason*. Translated by Lewis White Beck. IN: Bobbs-Merrill, 1956.

___. "The Metaphysics of Morals." In *Practical Philosophy: The Cambridge Edition of the Works of Immanuel Kant*, translated and edited by Mary J. Gregor, 370–540. Cambridge: Cambridge University Press, 1996.

Laidlaw, James. *The Subject of Virtue: An Anthropology of Ethics and Freedom*. Cambridge: Cambridge University Press, 2014.

Lambek, Michael, ed. *Ordinary Ethics: Anthropology, Language, and Action.* New York: Fordham University Press, 2010.

Mahmood, Saba. *Politics of Piety: The Islamic Revival and the Feminist Subject*. Princeton: Princeton University Press, 2005; reissue with a new preface by the author, 2012.

___. "Rehearsed Spontaneity and the Conventionality of Ritual: Disciplines of Salat." *American Ethnologist* vol. 28, issue 4 (2008): 827–53.

___. "Religious Freedom, the Minority Question, and Geopolitics in the Middle East." *Comparative Studies in Society and History* 15 (2) (2012): 418–46.

___. "Sectarian Conflict and Family Law in Egypt." *American Ethnologist* 39 (1) (2012): 54–62.

Marcus, George and Michael Fischer, eds. *Anthropology as Cultural Critique: An Experimental Moment in the Human Sciences.* Chicago: University of Chicago Press, 1986.

Mittermaier, Amira. "Dreams from Elsewhere: Muslim Subjectivities Beyond the Trope of Self-cultivation." *Journal of the Royal Anthropological Institute* 18, no. 2 (2012): 247–65.

Povinelli, Elizabeth A. *Economies of Abandonment: Social Belonging and Endurance in Late Liberalism.* Durham, NC: Duke University Press, 2011.

Schielke, Samuli. "Being Good in Ramadan: Ambivalence, Fragmentation, and the Moral Self in the Lives of Young Egyptians." *Journal of the Royal Anthropological Institute* 15, suppl. 1 (2009): S24–S40.

Tambiah, Stanley J. *A Performative Approach to Ritual.* London: The British Academy and Oxford University Press, 1979.

____. *Culture, Thought, and Social Action: An Anthropological Perspective.* Cambridge, Mass.: Harvard University Press, 1985.

Taylor, Charles. "Atomism." In *Philosophy and the Human Sciences: Philosophical Papers 2,* edited by Charles Taylor, 187–210. Cambridge: Cambridge University Press, 1985.

____. "What's Wrong with Negative Liberty?" In *Philosophy and the Human Sciences: Philosophical Papers 2,* edited by Charles Taylor, 211–29. Cambridge: Cambridge University Press, 1985.

Turner, Victor W. *The Ritual Process: Structure and Anti-Structure.* Chicago: Aldine Publishing Co., 1969.

THE MACAT LIBRARY
BY DISCIPLINE

AFRICANA STUDIES

Chinua Achebe's *An Image of Africa: Racism in Conrad's Heart of Darkness*
W. E. B. Du Bois's *The Souls of Black Folk*
Zora Neale Huston's *Characteristics of Negro Expression*
Martin Luther King Jr's *Why We Can't Wait*
Toni Morrison's *Playing in the Dark: Whiteness in the American Literary Imagination*

ANTHROPOLOGY

Arjun Appadurai's *Modernity at Large: Cultural Dimensions of Globalisation*
Philippe Ariès's *Centuries of Childhood*
Franz Boas's *Race, Language and Culture*
Kim Chan & Renée Mauborgne's *Blue Ocean Strategy*
Jared Diamond's *Guns, Germs & Steel: the Fate of Human Societies*
Jared Diamond's *Collapse: How Societies Choose to Fail or Survive*
E. E. Evans-Pritchard's *Witchcraft, Oracles and Magic Among the Azande*
James Ferguson's *The Anti-Politics Machine*
Clifford Geertz's *The Interpretation of Cultures*
David Graeber's *Debt: the First 5000 Years*
Karen Ho's *Liquidated: An Ethnography of Wall Street*
Geert Hofstede's *Culture's Consequences: Comparing Values, Behaviors, Institutes and Organizations across Nations*
Claude Lévi-Strauss's *Structural Anthropology*
Jay Macleod's *Ain't No Makin' It: Aspirations and Attainment in a Low-Income Neighborhood*
Saba Mahmood's *The Politics of Piety: The Islamic Revival and the Feminist Subject*
Marcel Mauss's *The Gift*

BUSINESS

Jean Lave & Etienne Wenger's *Situated Learning*
Theodore Levitt's *Marketing Myopia*
Burton G. Malkiel's *A Random Walk Down Wall Street*
Douglas McGregor's *The Human Side of Enterprise*
Michael Porter's *Competitive Strategy: Creating and Sustaining Superior Performance*
John Kotter's *Leading Change*
C. K. Prahalad & Gary Hamel's *The Core Competence of the Corporation*

CRIMINOLOGY

Michelle Alexander's *The New Jim Crow: Mass Incarceration in the Age of Colorblindness*
Michael R. Gottfredson & Travis Hirschi's *A General Theory of Crime*
Richard Herrnstein & Charles A. Murray's *The Bell Curve: Intelligence and Class Structure in American Life*
Elizabeth Loftus's *Eyewitness Testimony*
Jay Macleod's *Ain't No Makin' It: Aspirations and Attainment in a Low-Income Neighborhood*
Philip Zimbardo's *The Lucifer Effect*

ECONOMICS

Janet Abu-Lughod's *Before European Hegemony*
Ha-Joon Chang's *Kicking Away the Ladder*
David Brion Davis's *The Problem of Slavery in the Age of Revolution*
Milton Friedman's *The Role of Monetary Policy*
Milton Friedman's *Capitalism and Freedom*
David Graeber's *Debt: the First 5000 Years*
Friedrich Hayek's *The Road to Serfdom*
Karen Ho's *Liquidated: An Ethnography of Wall Street*

The Macat Library By Discipline

John Maynard Keynes's *The General Theory of Employment, Interest and Money*
Charles P. Kindleberger's *Manias, Panics and Crashes*
Robert Lucas's *Why Doesn't Capital Flow from Rich to Poor Countries?*
Burton G. Malkiel's *A Random Walk Down Wall Street*
Thomas Robert Malthus's *An Essay on the Principle of Population*
Karl Marx's *Capital*
Thomas Piketty's *Capital in the Twenty-First Century*
Amartya Sen's *Development as Freedom*
Adam Smith's *The Wealth of Nations*
Nassim Nicholas Taleb's *The Black Swan: The Impact of the Highly Improbable*
Amos Tversky's & Daniel Kahneman's *Judgment under Uncertainty: Heuristics and Biases*
Mahbub Ul Haq's *Reflections on Human Development*
Max Weber's *The Protestant Ethic and the Spirit of Capitalism*

FEMINISM AND GENDER STUDIES

Judith Butler's *Gender Trouble*
Simone De Beauvoir's *The Second Sex*
Michel Foucault's *History of Sexuality*
Betty Friedan's *The Feminine Mystique*
Saba Mahmood's *The Politics of Piety: The Islamic Revival and the Feminist Subjec*t
Joan Wallach Scott's *Gender and the Politics of History*
Mary Wollstonecraft's *A Vindication of the Rights of Woman*
Virginia Woolf's *A Room of One's Own*

GEOGRAPHY

The Brundtland Report's *Our Common Future*
Rachel Carson's *Silent Spring*
Charles Darwin's *On the Origin of Species*
James Ferguson's *The Anti-Politics Machine*
Jane Jacobs's *The Death and Life of Great American Cities*
James Lovelock's *Gaia: A New Look at Life on Earth*
Amartya Sen's *Development as Freedom*
Mathis Wackernagel & William Rees's *Our Ecological Footprint*

HISTORY

Janet Abu-Lughod's *Before European Hegemony*
Benedict Anderson's *Imagined Communities*
Bernard Bailyn's *The Ideological Origins of the American Revolution*
Hanna Batatu's *The Old Social Classes And The Revolutionary Movements Of Iraq*
Christopher Browning's *Ordinary Men: Reserve Police Batallion 101 and the Final Solution in Poland*
Edmund Burke's *Reflections on the Revolution in France*
William Cronon's *Nature's Metropolis: Chicago And The Great West*
Alfred W. Crosby's *The Columbian Exchange*
Hamid Dabashi's *Iran: A People Interrupted*
David Brion Davis's *The Problem of Slavery in the Age of Revolution*
Nathalie Zemon Davis's *The Return of Martin Guerre*
Jared Diamond's *Guns, Germs & Steel: the Fate of Human Societies*
Frank Dikotter's *Mao's Great Famine*
John W Dower's *War Without Mercy: Race And Power In The Pacific War*
W. E. B. Du Bois's *The Souls of Black Folk*
Richard J. Evans's *In Defence of History*
Lucien Febvre's *The Problem of Unbelief in the 16th Century*
Sheila Fitzpatrick's *Everyday Stalinism*

Eric Foner's *Reconstruction: America's Unfinished Revolution, 1863-1877*
Michel Foucault's *Discipline and Punish*
Michel Foucault's *History of Sexuality*
Francis Fukuyama's *The End of History and the Last Man*
John Lewis Gaddis's *We Now Know: Rethinking Cold War History*
Ernest Gellner's *Nations and Nationalism*
Eugene Genovese's *Roll, Jordan, Roll: The World the Slaves Made*
Carlo Ginzburg's *The Night Battles*
Daniel Goldhagen's *Hitler's Willing Executioners*
Jack Goldstone's *Revolution and Rebellion in the Early Modern World*
Antonio Gramsci's *The Prison Notebooks*
Alexander Hamilton, John Jay & James Madison's *The Federalist Papers*
Christopher Hill's *The World Turned Upside Down*
Carole Hillenbrand's *The Crusades: Islamic Perspectives*
Thomas Hobbes's *Leviathan*
Eric Hobsbawm's *The Age Of Revolution*
John A. Hobson's *Imperialism: A Study*
Albert Hourani's *History of the Arab Peoples*
Samuel P. Huntington's *The Clash of Civilizations and the Remaking of World Order*
C. L. R. James's *The Black Jacobins*
Tony Judt's *Postwar: A History of Europe Since 1945*
Ernst Kantorowicz's *The King's Two Bodies: A Study in Medieval Political Theology*
Paul Kennedy's *The Rise and Fall of the Great Powers*
Ian Kershaw's *The "Hitler Myth": Image and Reality in the Third Reich*
John Maynard Keynes's *The General Theory of Employment, Interest and Money*
Charles P. Kindleberger's *Manias, Panics and Crashes*
Martin Luther King Jr's *Why We Can't Wait*
Henry Kissinger's *World Order: Reflections on the Character of Nations and the Course of History*
Thomas Kuhn's *The Structure of Scientific Revolutions*
Georges Lefebvre's *The Coming of the French Revolution*
John Locke's *Two Treatises of Government*
Niccolò Machiavelli's *The Prince*
Thomas Robert Malthus's *An Essay on the Principle of Population*
Mahmood Mamdani's *Citizen and Subject: Contemporary Africa And The Legacy Of Late Colonialism*
Karl Marx's *Capital*
Stanley Milgram's *Obedience to Authority*
John Stuart Mill's *On Liberty*
Thomas Paine's *Common Sense*
Thomas Paine's *Rights of Man*
Geoffrey Parker's *Global Crisis: War, Climate Change and Catastrophe in the Seventeenth Century*
Jonathan Riley-Smith's *The First Crusade and the Idea of Crusading*
Jean-Jacques Rousseau's *The Social Contract*
Joan Wallach Scott's *Gender and the Politics of History*
Theda Skocpol's *States and Social Revolutions*
Adam Smith's *The Wealth of Nations*
Timothy Snyder's *Bloodlands: Europe Between Hitler and Stalin*
Sun Tzu's *The Art of War*
Keith Thomas's *Religion and the Decline of Magic*
Thucydides's *The History of the Peloponnesian War*
Frederick Jackson Turner's *The Significance of the Frontier in American History*
Odd Arne Westad's *The Global Cold War: Third World Interventions And The Making Of Our Times*

The Macat Library By Discipline

LITERATURE

Chinua Achebe's *An Image of Africa: Racism in Conrad's Heart of Darkness*
Roland Barthes's *Mythologies*
Homi K. Bhabha's *The Location of Culture*
Judith Butler's *Gender Trouble*
Simone De Beauvoir's *The Second Sex*
Ferdinand De Saussure's *Course in General Linguistics*
T. S. Eliot's *The Sacred Wood: Essays on Poetry and Criticism*
Zora Neale Huston's *Characteristics of Negro Expression*
Toni Morrison's *Playing in the Dark: Whiteness in the American Literary Imagination*
Edward Said's *Orientalism*
Gayatri Chakravorty Spivak's *Can the Subaltern Speak?*
Mary Wollstonecraft's *A Vindication of the Rights of Women*
Virginia Woolf's *A Room of One's Own*

PHILOSOPHY

Elizabeth Anscombe's *Modern Moral Philosophy*
Hannah Arendt's *The Human Condition*
Aristotle's *Metaphysics*
Aristotle's *Nicomachean Ethics*
Edmund Gettier's *Is Justified True Belief Knowledge?*
Georg Wilhelm Friedrich Hegel's *Phenomenology of Spirit*
David Hume's *Dialogues Concerning Natural Religion*
David Hume's *The Enquiry for Human Understanding*
Immanuel Kant's *Religion within the Boundaries of Mere Reason*
Immanuel Kant's *Critique of Pure Reason*
Søren Kierkegaard's *The Sickness Unto Death*
Søren Kierkegaard's *Fear and Trembling*
C. S. Lewis's *The Abolition of Man*
Alasdair MacIntyre's *After Virtue*
Marcus Aurelius's *Meditations*
Friedrich Nietzsche's *On the Genealogy of Morality*
Friedrich Nietzsche's *Beyond Good and Evil*
Plato's *Republic*
Plato's *Symposium*
Jean-Jacques Rousseau's *The Social Contract*
Gilbert Ryle's *The Concept of Mind*
Baruch Spinoza's *Ethics*
Sun Tzu's *The Art of War*
Ludwig Wittgenstein's *Philosophical Investigations*

POLITICS

Benedict Anderson's *Imagined Communities*
Aristotle's *Politics*
Bernard Bailyn's *The Ideological Origins of the American Revolution*
Edmund Burke's *Reflections on the Revolution in France*
John C. Calhoun's *A Disquisition on Government*
Ha-Joon Chang's *Kicking Away the Ladder*
Hamid Dabashi's *Iran: A People Interrupted*
Hamid Dabashi's *Theology of Discontent: The Ideological Foundation of the Islamic Revolution in Iran*
Robert Dahl's *Democracy and its Critics*
Robert Dahl's *Who Governs?*
David Brion Davis's *The Problem of Slavery in the Age of Revolution*

Alexis De Tocqueville's *Democracy in America*
James Ferguson's *The Anti-Politics Machine*
Frank Dikotter's *Mao's Great Famine*
Sheila Fitzpatrick's *Everyday Stalinism*
Eric Foner's *Reconstruction: America's Unfinished Revolution, 1863-1877*
Milton Friedman's *Capitalism and Freedom*
Francis Fukuyama's *The End of History and the Last Man*
John Lewis Gaddis's *We Now Know: Rethinking Cold War History*
Ernest Gellner's *Nations and Nationalism*
David Graeber's *Debt: the First 5000 Years*
Antonio Gramsci's *The Prison Notebooks*
Alexander Hamilton, John Jay & James Madison's *The Federalist Papers*
Friedrich Hayek's *The Road to Serfdom*
Christopher Hill's *The World Turned Upside Down*
Thomas Hobbes's *Leviathan*
John A. Hobson's *Imperialism: A Study*
Samuel P. Huntington's *The Clash of Civilizations and the Remaking of World Order*
Tony Judt's *Postwar: A History of Europe Since 1945*
David C. Kang's *China Rising: Peace, Power and Order in East Asia*
Paul Kennedy's *The Rise and Fall of Great Powers*
Robert Keohane's *After Hegemony*
Martin Luther King Jr.'s *Why We Can't Wait*
Henry Kissinger's *World Order: Reflections on the Character of Nations and the Course of History*
John Locke's *Two Treatises of Government*
Niccolò Machiavelli's *The Prince*
Thomas Robert Malthus's *An Essay on the Principle of Population*
Mahmood Mamdani's *Citizen and Subject: Contemporary Africa And The Legacy Of Late Colonialism*
Karl Marx's *Capital*
John Stuart Mill's *On Liberty*
John Stuart Mill's *Utilitarianism*
Hans Morgenthau's *Politics Among Nations*
Thomas Paine's *Common Sense*
Thomas Paine's *Rights of Man*
Thomas Piketty's *Capital in the Twenty-First Century*
Robert D. Putman's *Bowling Alone*
John Rawls's *Theory of Justice*
Jean-Jacques Rousseau's *The Social Contract*
Theda Skocpol's *States and Social Revolutions*
Adam Smith's *The Wealth of Nations*
Sun Tzu's *The Art of War*
Henry David Thoreau's *Civil Disobedience*
Thucydides's *The History of the Peloponnesian War*
Kenneth Waltz's *Theory of International Politics*
Max Weber's *Politics as a Vocation*
Odd Arne Westad's *The Global Cold War: Third World Interventions And The Making Of Our Times*

POSTCOLONIAL STUDIES

Roland Barthes's *Mythologies*
Frantz Fanon's *Black Skin, White Masks*
Homi K. Bhabha's *The Location of Culture*
Gustavo Gutiérrez's *A Theology of Liberation*
Edward Said's *Orientalism*
Gayatri Chakravorty Spivak's *Can the Subaltern Speak?*

PSYCHOLOGY

Gordon Allport's *The Nature of Prejudice*
Alan Baddeley & Graham Hitch's *Aggression: A Social Learning Analysis*
Albert Bandura's *Aggression: A Social Learning Analysis*
Leon Festinger's *A Theory of Cognitive Dissonance*
Sigmund Freud's *The Interpretation of Dreams*
Betty Friedan's *The Feminine Mystique*
Michael R. Gottfredson & Travis Hirschi's *A General Theory of Crime*
Eric Hoffer's *The True Believer: Thoughts on the Nature of Mass Movements*
William James's *Principles of Psychology*
Elizabeth Loftus's *Eyewitness Testimony*
A. H. Maslow's *A Theory of Human Motivation*
Stanley Milgram's *Obedience to Authority*
Steven Pinker's *The Better Angels of Our Nature*
Oliver Sacks's *The Man Who Mistook His Wife For a Hat*
Richard Thaler & Cass Sunstein's *Nudge: Improving Decisions About Health, Wealth and Happiness*
Amos Tversky's *Judgment under Uncertainty: Heuristics and Biases*
Philip Zimbardo's *The Lucifer Effect*

SCIENCE

Rachel Carson's *Silent Spring*
William Cronon's *Nature's Metropolis: Chicago And The Great West*
Alfred W. Crosby's *The Columbian Exchange*
Charles Darwin's *On the Origin of Species*
Richard Dawkin's *The Selfish Gene*
Thomas Kuhn's *The Structure of Scientific Revolutions*
Geoffrey Parker's *Global Crisis: War, Climate Change and Catastrophe in the Seventeenth Century*
Mathis Wackernagel & William Rees's *Our Ecological Footprint*

SOCIOLOGY

Michelle Alexander's *The New Jim Crow: Mass Incarceration in the Age of Colorblindness*
Gordon Allport's *The Nature of Prejudice*
Albert Bandura's *Aggression: A Social Learning Analysis*
Hanna Batatu's *The Old Social Classes And The Revolutionary Movements Of Iraq*
Ha-Joon Chang's *Kicking Away the Ladder*
W. E. B. Du Bois's *The Souls of Black Folk*
Émile Durkheim's *On Suicide*
Frantz Fanon's *Black Skin, White Masks*
Frantz Fanon's *The Wretched of the Earth*
Eric Foner's *Reconstruction: America's Unfinished Revolution, 1863-1877*
Eugene Genovese's *Roll, Jordan, Roll: The World the Slaves Made*
Jack Goldstone's *Revolution and Rebellion in the Early Modern World*
Antonio Gramsci's *The Prison Notebooks*
Richard Herrnstein & Charles A Murray's *The Bell Curve: Intelligence and Class Structure in American Life*
Eric Hoffer's *The True Believer: Thoughts on the Nature of Mass Movements*
Jane Jacobs's *The Death and Life of Great American Cities*
Robert Lucas's *Why Doesn't Capital Flow from Rich to Poor Countries?*
Jay Macleod's *Ain't No Makin' It: Aspirations and Attainment in a Low Income Neighborhood*
Elaine May's *Homeward Bound: American Families in the Cold War Era*
Douglas McGregor's *The Human Side of Enterprise*
C. Wright Mills's *The Sociological Imagination*

Thomas Piketty's *Capital in the Twenty-First Century*
Robert D. Putman's *Bowling Alone*
David Riesman's *The Lonely Crowd: A Study of the Changing American Character*
Edward Said's *Orientalism*
Joan Wallach Scott's *Gender and the Politics of History*
Theda Skocpol's *States and Social Revolutions*
Max Weber's *The Protestant Ethic and the Spirit of Capitalism*

THEOLOGY

Augustine's *Confessions*
Benedict's *Rule of St Benedict*
Gustavo Gutiérrez's *A Theology of Liberation*
Carole Hillenbrand's *The Crusades: Islamic Perspectives*
David Hume's *Dialogues Concerning Natural Religion*
Immanuel Kant's *Religion within the Boundaries of Mere Reason*
Ernst Kantorowicz's *The King's Two Bodies: A Study in Medieval Political Theology*
Søren Kierkegaard's *The Sickness Unto Death*
C. S. Lewis's *The Abolition of Man*
Saba Mahmood's *The Politics of Piety: The Islamic Revival and the Feminist Subject*
Baruch Spinoza's *Ethics*
Keith Thomas's *Religion and the Decline of Magic*

COMING SOON

Chris Argyris's *The Individual and the Organisation*
Seyla Benhabib's *The Rights of Others*
Walter Benjamin's *The Work Of Art in the Age of Mechanical Reproduction*
John Berger's *Ways of Seeing*
Pierre Bourdieu's *Outline of a Theory of Practice*
Mary Douglas's *Purity and Danger*
Roland Dworkin's *Taking Rights Seriously*
James G. March's *Exploration and Exploitation in Organisational Learning*
Ikujiro Nonaka's *A Dynamic Theory of Organizational Knowledge Creation*
Griselda Pollock's *Vision and Difference*
Amartya Sen's *Inequality Re-Examined*
Susan Sontag's *On Photography*
Yasser Tabbaa's *The Transformation of Islamic Art*
Ludwig von Mises's *Theory of Money and Credit*

The Macat Library By Discipline

Macat Disciplines

Access the greatest ideas and thinkers across entire disciplines, including

AFRICANA STUDIES

Chinua Achebe's *An Image of Africa: Racism in Conrad's Heart of Darkness*

W. E. B. Du Bois's *The Souls of Black Folk*

Zora Neale Hurston's *Characteristics of Negro Expression*

Martin Luther King Jr.'s *Why We Can't Wait*

Toni Morrison's *Playing in the Dark: Whiteness in the American Literary Imagination*

Macat analyses are available from all good bookshops and libraries.

Access hundreds of analyses through one, multimedia tool.

Macat Disciplines

Access the greatest ideas and thinkers across entire disciplines, including

MACAT

FEMINISM, GENDER AND QUEER STUDIES

Simone De Beauvoir's
The Second Sex

Michel Foucault's
History of Sexuality

Betty Friedan's
The Feminine Mystique

Saba Mahmood's
The Politics of Piety:
The Islamic Revival and
the Feminist Subject

Joan Wallach Scott's
Gender and the
Politics of History

Mary Wollstonecraft's
A Vindication of the
Rights of Woman

Virginia Woolf's
A Room of One's Own

Judith Butler's
Gender Trouble

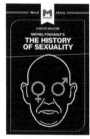

Macat analyses are available from all good bookshops and libraries.

Access hundreds of analyses through one, multimedia tool.

Join free for one month **library.macat.com**

Macat Disciplines

*Access the greatest ideas and thinkers
across entire disciplines, including*

INEQUALITY

Ha-Joon Chang's, *Kicking Away the Ladder*

David Graeber's, *Debt: The First 5000 Years*

Robert E. Lucas's, *Why Doesn't Capital Flow from
Rich To Poor Countries?*

Thomas Piketty's, *Capital in the Twenty-First Century*

Amartya Sen's, *Inequality Re-Examined*

Mahbub Ul Haq's, *Reflections on Human Development*

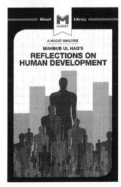

Macat analyses are available from all good bookshops and libraries.

Access hundreds of analyses through one, multimedia tool.
Join free for one month **library.macat.com**

Macat Disciplines

Access the greatest ideas and thinkers across entire disciplines, including

CRIMINOLOGY

Michelle Alexander's
The New Jim Crow: Mass Incarceration in the Age of Colorblindness

Michael R. Gottfredson & Travis Hirschi's
A General Theory of Crime

Elizabeth Loftus's
Eyewitness Testimony

Richard Herrnstein & Charles A. Murray's
The Bell Curve: Intelligence and Class Structure in American Life

Jay Macleod's
Ain't No Makin' It: Aspirations and Attainment in a Low-Income Neighborhood

Philip Zimbardo's
The Lucifer Effect

Macat analyses are available from all good bookshops and libraries.

Access hundreds of analyses through one, multimedia tool.

Join free for one month **libra**▓▓ **macat.com**

Macat Disciplines

Access the greatest ideas and thinkers across entire disciplines, including

Postcolonial Studies

Roland Barthes's *Mythologies*
Frantz Fanon's *Black Skin, White Masks*
Homi K. Bhabha's *The Location of Culture*
Gustavo Gutiérrez's *A Theology of Liberation*
Edward Said's *Orientalism*
Gayatri Chakravorty Spivak's *Can the Subaltern Speak?*

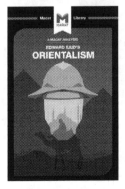

Macat analyses are available from all good bookshops and libraries.

Access hundreds of analyses through one, multimedia tool.
Join free for one month **library.macat.com**

Macat Disciplines

Access the greatest ideas and thinkers across entire disciplines, including

GLOBALIZATION

Arjun Appadurai's, *Modernity at Large: Cultural Dimensions of Globalisation*

James Ferguson's, *The Anti-Politics Machine*

Geert Hofstede's, *Culture's Consequences*

Amartya Sen's, *Development as Freedom*

Macat analyses are available from all good bookshops and libraries.

Access hundreds of analyses through one, multimedia tool. Join free for one month **library.macat.com**

Macat Pairs

Analyse historical and modern issues from opposite sides of an argument. Pairs include:

HOW TO RUN AN ECONOMY

John Maynard Keynes's
The General Theory OF Employment, Interest and Money

Classical economics suggests that market economies are self-correcting in times of recession or depression, and tend toward full employment and output. But English economist John Maynard Keynes disagrees.

In his ground-breaking 1936 study *The General Theory*, Keynes argues that traditional economics has misunderstood the causes of unemployment. Employment is not determined by the price of labor; it is directly linked to demand. Keynes believes market economies are by nature unstable, and so require government intervention. Spurred on by the social catastrophe of the Great Depression of the 1930s, he sets out to revolutionize the way the world thinks

Milton Friedman's
The Role of Monetary Policy

Friedman's 1968 paper changed the course of economic theory. In just 17 pages, he demolished existing theory and outlined an effective alternate monetary policy designed to secure 'high employment, stable prices and rapid growth.'

Friedman demonstrated that monetary policy plays a vital role in broader economic stability and argued that economists got their monetary policy wrong in the 1950s and 1960s by misunderstanding the relationship between inflation and unemployment. Previous generations of economists had believed that governments could permanently decrease unemployment by permitting inflation—and vice versa. Friedman's most original contribution was to show that this supposed trade-off is an illusion that only works in the short term.

Macat analyses are available from all good bookshops and libraries.

Access hundreds of analyses through one, multimedia tool.
Join free for one month **library.macat.com**

Macat Disciplines

Access the greatest ideas and thinkers across entire disciplines, including

THE FUTURE OF DEMOCRACY

Robert A. Dahl's, *Democracy and Its Critics*
Robert A. Dahl's, *Who Governs?*
Alexis De Toqueville's, *Democracy in America*
Niccolò Machiavelli's, *The Prince*
John Stuart Mill's, *On Liberty*
Robert D. Putnam's, *Bowling Alone*
Jean-Jacques Rousseau's, *The Social Contract*
Henry David Thoreau's, *Civil Disobedience*

Macat Pairs

*Analyse historical and modern issues
from opposite sides of an argument.
Pairs include:*

RACE AND IDENTITY

Zora Neale Hurston's
Characteristics of Negro Expression

Using material collected on anthropological
expeditions to the South, Zora Neale Hurston explains
how expression in African American culture in the
early twentieth century departs from the art of white
America. At the time, African American art was often
criticized for copying white culture. For Hurston, this
criticism misunderstood how art works. European
tradition views art as something fixed. But Hurston
describes a creative process that is alive, ever-
changing, and largely improvisational. She maintains
that African American art works through a process
called 'mimicry'—where an imitated object or verbal
pattern, for example, is reshaped and altered until
it becomes something new, novel—and worthy of
attention.

Frantz Fanon's
Black Skin, White Masks

Black Skin, White Masks offers a radical analysis of the
psychological effects of colonization on the colonized.

Fanon witnessed the effects of colonization first
hand both in his birthplace, Martinique, and again
later in life when he worked as a psychiatrist
in another French colony, Algeria. His text is
uncompromising in form and argument. He
dissects the dehumanizing effects of colonialism,
arguing that it destroys the native sense of identity,
forcing people to adapt to an alien set of values—
including a core belief that they are inferior. This
results in deep psychological trauma.

Fanon's work played a pivotal role in the civil rights
movements of the 1960s.

Macat analyses are available from all good bookshops and libraries.

Access hundreds of analyses through one, multimedia tool.
Join free for one month **library.macat.com**

Macat Pairs

Analyse historical and modern issues from opposite sides of an argument. Pairs include:

INTERNATIONAL RELATIONS IN THE 21ST CENTURY

Samuel P. Huntington's
The Clash of Civilisations

In his highly influential 1996 book, Huntington offers a vision of a post-Cold War world in which conflict takes place not between competing ideologies but between cultures. The worst clash, he argues, will be between the Islamic world and the West: the West's arrogance and belief that its culture is a "gift" to the world will come into conflict with Islam's obstinacy and concern that its culture is under attack from a morally decadent "other."

Clash inspired much debate between different political schools of thought. But its greatest impact came in helping define American foreign policy in the wake of the 2001 terrorist attacks in New York and Washington.

Francis Fukuyama's
The End of History and the Last Man

Published in 1992, *The End of History and the Last Man* argues that capitalist democracy is the final destination for all societies. Fukuyama believed democracy triumphed during the Cold War because it lacks the "fundamental contradictions" inherent in communism and satisfies our yearning for freedom and equality. Democracy therefore marks the endpoint in the evolution of ideology, and so the "end of history." There will still be "events," but no fundamental change in ideology.

Macat Disciplines

*Access the greatest ideas and thinkers
across entire disciplines, including*

MAN AND THE ENVIRONMENT

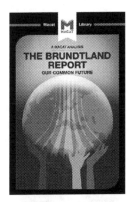

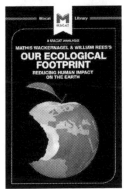

The Brundtland Report's, *Our Common Future*
Rachel Carson's, *Silent Spring*
James Lovelock's, *Gaia: A New Look at Life on Earth*
Mathis Wackernagel & William Rees's, *Our Ecological Footprint*

Macat analyses are available from all good bookshops and libraries.

Access hundreds of analyses through one, multimedia tool.
Join free for one month **library.macat.com**

Macat Pairs

Analyse historical and modern issues from opposite sides of an argument. Pairs include:

Macat Pairs

Analyse historical and modern issues from opposite sides of an argument. Pairs include:

HOW WE RELATE TO EACH OTHER AND SOCIETY

Jean-Jacques Rousseau's
The Social Contract

Rousseau's famous work sets out the radical concept of the 'social contract': a give-and-take relationship between individual freedom and social order.

If people are free to do as they like, governed only by their own sense of justice, they are also vulnerable to chaos and violence. To avoid this, Rousseau proposes, they should agree to give up some freedom to benefit from the protection of social and political organization. But this deal is only just if societies are led by the collective needs and desires of the people, and able to control the private interests of individuals. For Rousseau, the only legitimate form of government is rule by the people.

Robert D. Putnam's
Bowling Alone

In *Bowling Alone*, Robert Putnam argues that Americans have become disconnected from one another and from the institutions of their common life, and investigates the consequences of this change.

Looking at a range of indicators, from membership in formal organizations to the number of invitations being extended to informal dinner parties, Putnam demonstrates that Americans are interacting less and creating less "social capital" – with potentially disastrous implications for their society.

It would be difficult to overstate the impact of *Bowling Alone*, one of the most frequently cited social science publications of the last half-century.

Macat analyses are available from all good bookshops and libraries.

Access hundreds of analyses through one, multimedia tool.
Join free for one month **library.macat.com**

Printed in the United States
by Baker & Taylor Publisher Services